Mens et Mania

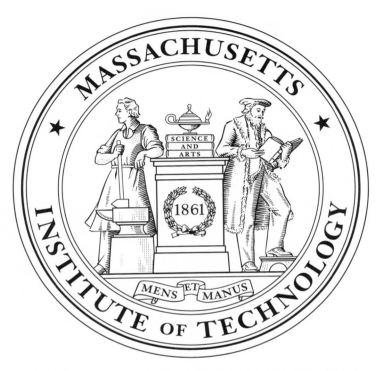

The MIT seal was adopted on the day after Christmas in 1864. Meant to convey that MIT is an institution devoted to knowledge and practice, the seal depicts a craftsman at an anvil and a scholar rapt in a book. The motto, *Mens et Manus* ("Mind and Hand"), flows across the banner below. I have always found it odd that *mens*—"mind"—is beneath the craftsman and *manus*—"hand"—beneath the scholar. But it is the thought that counts.

Mens et Mania

The MIT Nobody Knows

Samuel Jay Keyser

foreword by Lawrence S. Bacow

The MIT Press
Cambridge, Massachusetts
London, England

For information about special quantity discounts, please email special_sales@mitpress.mit.edu

This book was set in Stone Sans and Stone Serif by the MIT Press. Printed and bound in the United States of America.

Library of Congress Cataloging-in-Publication Data

Keyser, Samuel Jay, 1935–
Mens et mania : the MIT nobody knows / Samuel Jay Keyser ; foreword by Lawrence S. Bacow.
  p. cm.
ISBN 978-0-262-01594-3 (hardcover : alk. paper)
1. Keyser, Samuel Jay, 1935– 2. Massachusetts Institute of Technology—Faculty—Biography. 3. College department heads—Massachusetts—Cambridge—Biography. 4. Massachusetts Institute of Technology. Dept. of Linguistics and Philosophy. 5. Linguistics—Study and teaching (Higher)—Massachusetts—Cambridge. 6. College administrators—Massachusetts—Cambridge—Biography. 7. Massachusetts Institute of Technology. 8. Cambridge (Mass.)—Intellectual life. 9. Cambridge (Mass.)—Biography. I. Title
T171.M49K3   2011
378.744'4—dc22
[B]   2010043143

10 9 8 7 6 5 4 3 2 1

To Morris Halle,
colleague, mentor, and friend
for over half a century

Contents

Foreword

By any metric, MIT is a special place. Widely regarded as one of the finest universities in the world, MIT is, in the words of its former president James Killian, "a university polarized around science, engineering, and the arts." MIT students, faculty, and staff have won a total of 75 Nobel Prizes. MIT alumni have founded over 25,000 active companies that employ approximately 3.3 million people and generate worldwide sales of $2 trillion. If all the companies founded by MIT alumni formed an independent nation, their economy alone would be the seventeenth largest in the world.

MIT as an institution commands an unusual amount of respect from the public at large. Indeed, it is common when people refer to a particularly mentally challenging activity to say, "You need an MIT degree to do that." It is never a Harvard, Stanford, Caltech, or Yale degree. It is always an MIT degree.

From 1998 through 2001, I was privileged to serve as the chancellor of MIT. As chancellor, I was responsible for, among other things, MIT's international partnerships. During that period, it seemed that not a month would go by in which I was not approached by some head of state asking whether we would assist in replicating MIT in another part of the world. It seemed

that everyone wanted their own version of MIT, recognizing
that a world-class institution of science and technology could
act as a powerful stimulus for economic growth.

Many countries and many institutions have tried to replicate the success of the world's foremost institution for science
and technology. However, MIT is more than just a collection of
buildings on the Charles River populated by brilliant students,
faculty, and staff. MIT represents a particularly unique and often
poorly understood culture. Anyone who seeks to replicate or simply understand MIT must first try to understand and appreciate a
culture that celebrates quirkiness, choice, independence, entre-
preneurship, focus, creativity, and intensity. As Brian Hughes,
former president of the Alumni Association, observed, interesting things happen at MIT when faculty and students are con-
fined under temperature and pressure. I believe the MIT culture
acts as an important catalyst in this reaction.

In this book, Jay Keyser explores this culture from a truly
unique vantage point. In his long career at MIT, Jay has been
a faculty member, department chair, housemaster, and senior
academic administrator. He has truly lived among the natives
and understands and appreciates the MIT student culture as few
do. He brings a loving appreciation of all that makes MIT great,
together with a critical eye for all that makes MIT so challenging.
Anyone who cares about the Institute or wants to understand it
will appreciate this insightful book.

Lawrence S. Bacow, President
Tufts University

Acknowledgments

I would like to acknowledge first and foremost someone who will never see this acknowledgment. Constantine Simonides was vice president of MIT when I became its associate provost for educational programs and policy. Charles M. Vest in his book Pursuing the Endless Frontier described him as "a remarkable MIT administrator and a spiritual force at the Institute." For me Constantine was a Virgil to my poor man's Dante, only the tour never made it to heaven. I wish I could thank him for all the wisdom, insight, humanity, humor, pathos, bathos, cunning, and common sense that he left me with in my office around the corner. Unhappily, this will have to do.

Paul E. Gray, the fourteenth president of MIT, was gracious enough not only to read the manuscript but also to spend several hours in conversation with me, correcting my errors and nodding patiently when our views diverged. I was always an admirer of his while he was president of MIT. After writing this book, I have become an even stronger one.

Thanks also to Paul's successor, Charles M. Vest, for finding time that I am sure he could ill afford to spare to read the manuscript and to give me the benefit of his own insights. At one point Chuck commented that I was writing about the MIT within MIT. I think he nailed it. I am especially grateful to him for giving me a sense of how personally he felt the loss of Scott Krueger, the freshman who died at a fraternity initiation rite in September 1997. He suggested that he might someday write a book about those days. I certainly hope he does.

Larry Bacow read the manuscript carefully and encouraged me to write about the student culture at MIT. I have always had strong feelings about that. Larry gave me the courage to voice them. My thanks to him for that and for much else.

Robert Birgeneau found the time to read the manuscript on a flight from Taiwan to Japan. Thank goodness the flight was long enough. Bob's astute and savvy insights and his probing questions will keep me thinking about MIT for the next decade. I thank him for that gift.

Steve Lerman, who left MIT in July 2010 to become provost at my old alma mater, George Washington University, took time during his last days at MIT when he had many more pressing matters to deal with to read the manuscript and enrich it with his comments and observations. I am grateful for his wisdom and his generosity.

Without John Deutch there would have been no book. John appointed me associate provost in 1985 and essentially opened the door to a life of crisis management that I had no idea existed at MIT. I am grateful to John for that—I think. John read an early version of the manuscript and worried that it short-changed MIT's greatness as a research and educational institution. It may well be guilty of that. As Chuck Vest said, I am talking about the MIT within MIT. In any event, for better or for worse this is the book I chose to write.

This book is replete with material that I thought had long since disappeared. I was able to find it because of the diligence and expertise of the staff at the Institute Archives and Special

Collections. I would like to thank them all: Elizabeth Andrews, Ewa Basinska, Lois Beattie, Myles Crowley, Mikki Simon Macdonald, Silvia Mejia, Jeff Mifflin, Nora Murphy, Stephen Skuce, Craig Thomas, and especially the head of the archives, Tom Rosko, whose flexible management style made it possible for me to spend the summer of 2009 in his reading room. I could not have done this book without them. And a gentle thank you to Fiona, Tom Rosko's daughter, whose sunny disposition lightened the archives whenever she visited her father.

I would also like to thank a number of people who spoke with me about events that I did not witness first hand but in whose aftermath I was caught up. Steve Immerman, Henry (Jake) Jacoby, Robert Randolph, Ron Suduiko, and Kim Vandiver have been especially forthcoming and frank. Yonald Chery sharpened my recollection of the Project XL incident recounted in the preface. Keri Garel, a Senior House devotee and resident, deserves warm thanks for her candid discussion about where the heart and soul of Senior House lies in 2010, as does Ian Eslick for his assessment of what is really valuable at MIT—the students. I am in their debt. Finally, I would like to thank Jinane Dahleh and her spouse, Munther Dahleh, for going back to that day on April 9, 1986, when she screamed at me and for sharing their memories of what happened next.

Three close friends with whom I have shared ideas deserve special acknowledgment: Ellen Harris, Philip Khoury, and Rosalind Williams. Along with Larry Bacow and Robert Birgeneau we have formed a kind of twice-a-year luncheon club. These lunches have been to me what the Algonquin Round Table must have been to Harpo Marx. My thanks to all of you for your wit, your insights about MIT, and most of all, your company.

Speaking of company, the members of the Moses Seminar have been my intellectual companions for well over a quarter of a century. They include the seminar's namesake, Joel Moses, its current majordomo, Arthur Steinberg, and its faithful members, Robert Berwick, Fernando Corbato, Randy Davis, Robert Fano, Gadi Geiger, Alan Guth, Hyman Hartman, Steve Lerman, Seth Lloyd, Andrew Lo, Silvio Micali, David Mindell, Sanjoy Mitter, Ron Rivest, David Staelin, Gil Strang, Gerry Sussman, David Warsh, and Patrick Winston. Over the years their experience, wisdom, and penetrating analyses of everything from quantum computers to general Institute requirements have informed and honed my love for what Paul Gray calls "this special place, MIT."

I would like to acknowledge by name all the members of Portia with whom I have worked for the past quarter of a century. But to do that would blow their cover. It will have to suffice for me to say that their collective wisdom over the years has been as much a teacher for me as a source of pleasure. I thank all of them anonymously for that. They will know who they are.

I want to thank Michael Strauss, a friend for over a quarter of a century. An MIT undergraduate and PhD, Mike has hashed and rehashed many of the issues touched on in this book. I thank him for his probing questions, his infinite patience as a listener, and his steady judgment.

I would like to thank Wendy Strothman, whose advice, always free, was also always right on. If getting what you pay for is the rule, Wendy is the exception that tests it.

Gita Devi Manaktala, the editorial director of MIT Press, has been incredibly supportive and helpful. Her suggestions for changes and revisions have made this a better book. But most of all I am grateful for her patience as I swung back and forth like a child on a swing trying to decide what to do next.

I would like to thank Jerry Weinstein, one of MIT's many able lawyers at Palmer and Dodge—the others that I worked with over the years were Thane Scott, Robert Sullivan, and Jeff Swope—who first became a colleague and then a personal friend. I have shared this manuscript with him and his support and advice have been, as they always were, invaluable.

I have worked with Deborah Chasman on two books. This is the second. Each one she has made better because of her remarkable skills as an editor and as someone who sees the big picture. "Thank you" seems quite feeble against her contribution to teaching me how to be a better writer.

Through no fault of my own, this book was assigned to a freelance copy editor named Anne Mark. Truth in advertising: Anne and I have worked together for forty years in producing a journal that I edit called Linguistic Inquiry. She has acquired the reputation of being the best copy editor in the field of linguistics. I would emend that judgment slightly by eliminating the final two words of the last sentence. I count it an extraordinary stroke of luck that Anne was able and willing to copyedit this book. It is a marriage made in writer's heaven.

Finally, my wife, Nancy, has listened to me reading aloud from this book enough times to test any marriage. I needed her approval and she never stinted in granting it. Without her constant support, I doubt this book would ever have seen the light of day.

If I were to make a thorough list of the people who deserve recognition for making my academic life fun, interesting, and even worthwhile, that list would have had to be as long as this book, even longer. As John Donne said, "No man is an island." Let me end by asking the forgiveness of the many people whose wisdom and good sense made it possible for me to write this remembrance of my life as a scholar and an administrator and whose names are, like ghosted notes in a melody, only felt.

Preface

The students who were scheduled to see me arrived promptly at 10 a.m. My secretary ushered them into the office. I motioned toward a small round table I used for appointments. I rarely talked to visitors across the proscenium arch that was my desk. It was one of the original library reading desks designed by William Bosworth to fit the inside curvature of his signature MIT landmark, the Great Dome. There weren't a lot of those desks in circulation. I grabbed at the chance to have one about to be put out to pasture. It was a lovely desk, made of cherry wood, gently curving outward like the leading wave in a pond after a pebble has been dropped. Even so, it put the kibosh on easy conversations about touchy subjects.

The occasion for this meeting was touchy. All meetings having to do with diversity at MIT were, especially after the anti-apartheid demonstrations that rocked the Institute in March 1986. Now, two years later, the issue was Project Interphase, a program meant to help minority students make the transition from high school to MIT.

This day's meeting came after fifty minority students had staged a demonstration on the steps of the entrance to MIT, also designed by William Bosworth. The demonstration had been a silent one broken by three speeches declaring the students' griev-ances. The details of the grievances don't matter. It's enough to say that they added up to reducing the number of choices available to the program's students. To make matters worse, the dean for student affairs had announced the changes without stu-dent consultation. Those are two huge red flags at MIT. Don't take away choice if you can possibly help it. If you can't, make damned sure you've talked with the students until both sides are blue in the face, regardless of the color of their skin.

The spokesman for the group was a young man named Yonald Chery. He was neither black nor white. He was, as he described himself, "of mixed race." He had made a practice of checking both white and black boxes on official forms that asked about race.

While a junior in high school, Yonald had been through the Minority Introduction to Engineering and Science (MITES), an MIT program designed to expose minority students to what an MIT education tastes like. His experience had been stellar. He left at the top of the class. When he was admitted to MIT the follow-ing year, he looked forward to Project Interphase, a parallel pro-gram for incoming freshmen to bring them up to speed. Unlike his MITES experience, Project Interphase was a disaster. Some of the Interphase tutors tried, as he put it, to "scare me straight" about how racist MIT was. For him the irony was that the racism seemed to come from the other direction. At one point he com-plained to the director of the program about an instructor who had referred to him as a "half-breed."

Yonald was not unknown to me when he came to see me, though I didn't know him very well. We had both been mem-bers of an important committee at the Institute, the Committee on Undergraduate Programs—he as a student representative, I as associate provost for educational programs and policy. I thought of him as someone committed to "working from within" to make things better for minorities. What I hadn't realized was how strongly committed he was. He was motivated by his bad experience with Project Interphase and a strong desire not to allow the program to be extended into the freshman year. That was what the dean for student affairs was proposing.

Prior to coming to see me, he had met with leaders from the Black Student Union as well as with a number of other interested parties. Over a period of weeks he and his student colleagues had worked out an alternative proposal. His visit was part of a strategy to put the new proposal on the table rather than be confronted with a fait accompli.

We had just sat down at my small round conference table when the door was pushed open and several uninvited visitors sauntered into the room, pulled up chairs, and sat down at the table with us. My heart sank. Among them were some of the radical students I had dealt with two years earlier. I hadn't counted on this. If I had to deal with them, then the whole enterprise had the potential of blowing up. Nothing I might do would be accepted at face value. There would be accusations in the student newspaper. I would be labeled a racist, a liar, a manipulator, anything necessary to start a fire and fan it. All that was tumbling through my mind in the few seconds it took for the students to arrange themselves around the table. I began making a mental list of possible tacks to take, how to put them out there, but before I could say a word, Yonald spoke up.

"What are you doing here?"

"We just want to sit in on the meeting," one of the other students answered nonchalantly.

I might as well have been in the next office over. If ever discretion were the better part of valor, it was now. I kept my mouth shut.

"That wasn't what we decided last night," Yonald replied. If I was apprehensive, he was irate.

"What's the problem? We just want to sit in on the meeting."

"Yeah. Well, this isn't about you," Yonald thrust back at them. "This is about what we voted on last night. We were the ones who would meet with Keyser. Not you."

I wasn't put off by the reference to me unadorned by "provost" or "professor" or even "mister." A senior administrator who expected that from an MIT student would be like a prison inmate expecting a birthday card from the warden.

"We're not leaving," said their spokesman.

These were the moments I dreaded as a senior administrator. Everything depended on what I did and, frankly, I hadn't a clue what the right thing might be. After all, there are no handbooks when you take jobs like this. You get where you are largely because of your expertise as a scholar—my field happened to be linguistics—but there is no discernible connection that I can see between being a linguist and being associate provost for educational programs and policy. I've often wondered if universities are unique in this regard. Upper-level managers, from department heads to provosts, aren't there because they are particularly good managers. In fact, I would venture to say that at least half, probably more, are not. They are there because the people who put them there thought they would be simpatico, easy to get along with.

Anyway, I had developed a fundamental principle of life: when in doubt, do nothing. I decided to apply it.

"Look," I said, getting up from the table, "it's up to you guys to decide who I'm meeting with. Why don't I just leave you to it. I'll wait outside in the hall."

I shut the office door behind me. My secretary looked puzzled.

"They're having a fight," I shrugged. "They're trying to decide who's in charge. I'll just walk around the corridor until they do. Tell whoever wins to come find me."

My office was just around the corner from the president's. I remember pacing up and down in front of his outer office wondering which faction would win. I had my fingers crossed that Yonald would, but I was dubious.

Just then Paul Gray, the fourteenth president of MIT, opened the door and stepped out into the corridor.

Seeing me pacing like a caged lion, he asked, "What's up?"

I told him, including the names of the students I'd left behind.

"You mean you left those students alone in your office?"

I'm not sure what was going through his mind. Perhaps he had recalled the Vietnam War protests when students and at least one faculty member had used a battering ram to break into the president's office fifteen years earlier when he was chancellor and Jerome Wiesner was president.

There have only been four chancellors in MIT's history, with big gaps separating the first three. Chancellor at MIT is an odd position, a kind of administrative U-Haul. It is higher than associate provost and lower than provost, the organization chart notwithstanding. Usually, the fiefdoms of the chancellor and the provost are worked out in advance, but with the provost always holding the purse strings. That's the measure of where the real power at MIT is: the one who controls the money tap. The great advantage of the position of chancellor is that it increases flexibility at the upper end of administrative appointments. It was created in 1956 to enable Julius Stratton to run MIT while James R. Killian, the tenth president of MIT, was serving in Washington as Dwight Eisenhower's science advisor. It was reinstated in 1971 to give Paul Gray a perch from which to oversee the MIT budget, something he was a master at, while Jerome Wiesner was president. Jerry was doing the vision thing. Paul controlled the costs. Now Paul was president, having succeeded Jerry Wiesner in 1980.

So the previous chancellor and now fourteenth president of MIT and I stood looking at one another for a long, silent moment. Then Paul shook his head in disbelief and walked off. I could just hear him asking himself, "What kind of administrator leaves his office in the hands of students?"

This was one of those times when you regretted that the president of MIT was so damned accessible.

Shortly after Paul left, Yonald came looking for me.

"Shall we meet?" he asked. He was grinning from ear to ear. Obviously, my guy won.

Subsequently, I arranged a meeting between Yonald and the dean for student affairs. To make a long story short, Yonald outlined the alternative proposal and gave it a name, Project XL. It was adopted. The following semester he was designated the program's assistant director. (He was still a student at the time.) Later he told me that thirty-three out of thirty-five students in Project XL passed all of their first-term courses. Of the two who didn't make it, one failed because he decided he would rather play golf.

Paul Gray wrote me a note shortly after the affair was settled. He said, "I think I have some sense of how much time, careful thought, and emotional energy were involved in bringing the highly charged discussions about Project Interphase to a happy conclusion last week. It is evident to me that you were the key individual in bringing these discussions to an outcome that satisfied the desire of our students to have their views heard and reflected the convictions of the faculty to do a better and more effective job with Project Interphase."

I asked Yonald many years later why he had come to me. After all, it wasn't my program. He said, "I thought you would be helpful in setting up a meeting with the appropriate parties. I saw you as a middleman."

His remark rang a bell. Much of my life at the Institute involved conflict resolution. In Yonald's case I got lucky. But most of the time I felt like a marriage counselor trying to reconcile a union between a Jehovah's Witness and a vampire.

This book is about those counseling sessions.

I Mens

1   The Wrecking Ball

On a mid-April day in 1999, almost nine months from the time I had formally retired from the faculty of MIT, I was walking along a path that took me behind Building 20. At MIT all buildings have numbers. Some are known by their numbers. Some are not. How they are divvied up is interesting. I'll get to that in the next-to-last chapter. For now let me say that Building 20 was the place where I spent seven years as head of the Department of Linguistics and Philosophy. The building was being demolished to make way for the new and soon-to-be-controversial Frank Gehry–designed Stata Center. I don't know what drew me there on that day in mid-April. I can't even remember where I was going. As I walked between Building 26 and the swimming pool, I looked up just in time to see a wrecking ball drive through my old office. In one swift second the room disappeared, replaced by a cloud of fifty-year-old dust and a maelstrom of splinters.

That, I think, was the moment that I finally left MIT, not so much in my mind, but in my heart. MIT is a hard place to leave. Coming to MIT as I did in 1977 to head the newly formed Department of Linguistics and Philosophy, I felt like a fish that had found its way to water for the first time. No wonder it took a wrecking ball to dislodge me.

A colleague once told me that the reason I held MIT in such high regard was that I conferred rock star status on my fellow faculty members. He said that I was harboring the illusion that if my colleagues were rock stars, then I must be one myself. This was a colleague who was, indeed, that good. He was also that cynical.

I don't think he was right, of course. I thought my assessment of my colleagues at MIT was simply accurate. I still think so. Roughly, every other faculty member you meet walking down an MIT corridor is worth talking to, a higher ratio than most places that have corridors. I remember an encounter with a colleague in Physics. He stopped me one afternoon in the middle of the Infinite Corridor, the longest unimpeded hallway at MIT. He told me that 98 percent of the matter in the universe is completely undetectable. Everything we know is based on just 2 percent of what's out there. That's all we can detect. Nothing else out there interacts with light.

"We can't see it. Do you realize how ignorant we are?" he asked, grasping my lapels.

"I do. I do," I said. I remember thinking how much I must have sounded like the Cowardly Lion in *The Wizard of Oz*.

He let me go.

I loved these encounters. Not, as my cynical colleague would have it, because they enhanced my view of how good I was—I am actually under no illusions about that—but because they underscored what it's like being in a community that contains people who grab one's lapels over dark matter rather than, say, vinyl siding.

It was not so far-fetched that I should hold my colleagues in such high regard. One of them was a man the *Village Voice* once described as "arguably the most important intellectual alive."

That would be Noam Chomsky. I was his department head for seven years. During my stint Noam insisted on calling me "Boss."

One day I buttonholed him in the corridor.

"I finally figured out why you call me boss," I told him.

He looked quizzical.

"It's because 'boss' is double-S O B spelled backwards."

Noam has never actually denied it.

The building I watched buckling under the fist of the wrecking ball was the building where I had spent my formative years at MIT. It was erected in December 1943 as a temporary structure to house research on microwave radar during World War II. It was supposed to come down six months after the war ended. That would have put its demise at February 15, 1946, half a year after the Japanese surrender. Fifty-three years later the building was still standing. It would still be standing were it not for an MIT administration that believed that the intellectual ethos of an institution ought to be reflected in its architecture.

Known during the last year before its destruction as "that rat's nest of a building," in its death it was hailed as "The Magic Incubator." Why the relabeling? Perhaps the Institute felt a guilty pang at having brought down one of the most creative edifices in its long history of creativity. Building 20 was the home of the Radiation Laboratory where during World War II its development of radar contributed more than anything else, save the atomic bomb, toward winning the war. It was the home of the Chomskyan revolution in linguistics, establishing for the first time a firm theoretical basis for the scientific study of the human mind.

In the early 1960s a group of Russian scientists visited the building. One of my oldest friends and colleagues was their host. He was working on a device that could generate human speech sounds, the kind of work that led to those robotlike answering services that tell you to push 1 if you want to buy something. After a tour of his Building 20 laboratory, my friend asked one of the Russians why they were working on speech recognition.

"Because you are," he answered in a splendid moment of candor. That work, in fact, is one of the major themes in Solzhenitsyn's *The First Circle*. In the novel, prisoners are forced to do the same research inside a special Moscow prison "institute" that my friend was doing inside the Massachusetts Institute of Technology's Building 20. Solzhenitsyn's choice of that word, "institute," was no accident.

Building 20 was a gray asbestos-sided wooden structure whose windows you could actually open yourself. The floor joists were strong enough to hold metal presses. The inner walls were movable. The office bays could be reshaped with the ease of a Lincoln log toy. It was a building whose flexibility harmonized with an attitude of mind that characterized the scientific thinking going on inside it. Be ready to change your point of view at a moment's notice. (It is ironic that what is highly valued in science, the ability to turn on a dime if the evidence warrants it, is called, in politics, flip-flopping.)

The Academic Council is MIT's highest policymaking body. As associate provost I sat on that body for nine years. At one of its meetings I was thunderstruck to hear the MIT provost, now head of one of the country's great academic institutions, argue that Building 20 was a rat's nest that needed to come down. To my mind, tearing down Building 20 would be like draining Walden Pond. My colleagues around the council table warmly received the provost's remarks. It was as if they all owned stock in a wrecking ball company. They couldn't have been more wrong, I thought. None of them had ever lived in Building 20. Those who did understood that you can't tell a book by its cover.

Building 20 represented the old soul of MIT. The spirit of that soul was captured in a remark Chomsky made to a visiting delegation from Japan. The delegation had come in through the pitted, unpainted doors on Vassar Street. A single trash can stood outside like a dilapidated R2-D2 knockoff. It was the kind of trash can that had a miniature sandbox on top for cigarette butts and a trash- eating mouth. The delegation walked past the room just inside the entrance where a subsequent generation of students would put together one of the first solar electric powered commuter cars. They walked past the coffee-vending machine where, if it ate your quarter, a card above the slot told you to telephone Salvatore Lauricella. It even listed his telephone number. When you dialed, Sal answered. Not a recording. Your quarter arrived in the mail, no questions asked. Sal's widow—she still works at MIT—is a pleasant reminder of those days.

The party climbed the scarred but sturdy steps to the second floor where they found themselves in a long corridor with wooden floorboards worn thin by decades of Building 20 denizens pacing up and down trying to figure out their next theoretical move. Someone directed them to Chomsky's office. There were, of course, no signs. True to Building 20 fashion, his office was well lit with natural light flooding in through several windows that actually opened. The frames, warped and worn by years of weathering, admitted tiny hillocks of snow during winter storms. Not to worry. The winters, though long, weren't that long.

When the delegation came in, Chomsky rose to greet them, exposing a large pit in the foam rubber seat of his swivel chair. Large it was, but not so large as to be uncomfortable. The members of the delegation were the ones who were uncomfortable. Pointing to the drafty windows and the pitted seat, one of them asked, "Does MIT not respect linguistics?"

"Your office seems so neglected," they explained.

Noam reassured them. "Our motto is: Physically shabby. Intellectually first class."

Now that is the MIT I want to remember, the MIT before the wrecking ball splintered my office. Alas, it is gone. The end of the twentieth century and the beginning of the twenty-first has subjected the MIT campus to a *Queer Eye for the Straight Guy* makeover that is breathtaking. Its buildings win prizes. San Francisco look-alike rubber-wheeled trolleys filled with camera-toting tourists stop in front of them. The tourists have even begun to invade the halls of the Institute. They make their way to the president's office to peep in. They open the doors of laboratories for a look-see. Artsy photographers sell odd-angled photographs of the newest buildings on the Internet. Who would have thought it possible? Well, times change. But that doesn't mean that I have to change with them. I am willing to go so far but no farther. The death of Building 20 was where I drew the line.

MIT was the last stop for the railroad train that was my academic career. The first stop was at Brandeis University. From 1965 (when I was 30) to 1972 I headed a fledgling program in linguistics located in the English Department. From 1972 to 1977 I was head of the Department of Linguistics at the University of Massachusetts at Amherst. In 1977, at the age of 42, I became head of the Department of Linguistics and Philosophy at MIT. Starting in 1979, I was concurrently director of the Center for Cognitive Science. I was 50 years old in 1985 when I became associate provost at MIT, first "for educational programs and policy" and then with the more grandiose tag "for Institute life." In 1997 I was appointed special assistant to the chancellor. Finally, in 1998 I put an end to it all. At age 63 I retired from the faculty, though, at the request of the chancellor, I stayed on as special assistant, doing the odd job here and there. As I write this, I still hold that position.

There you have my thirty-three-year-long professional life in a paragraph. Always head of this, director of that, associate provost for something else. It was the life of someone who stood between the troops and their superiors, one leg in the trenches, the other in the corridors of power. Sound uncomfortable? Not for me. Administering was something I did without thinking twice. There were moments, of course, when the going was miserable, absolutely miserable. Most of this book will be about those moments. But for the most part being an administrator was a breeze.

In 1985 John Deutch, the newly named provost at the Institute, asked me to become associate provost. After a year on the job, in one of his no-beating-around-the-bush moods, John told me, "Jay, I may have put you in the administration, but you are definitely not of it."

John saw himself as doing me a favor by giving me a chance to see the way things worked at a great university from a vantage point that I would otherwise not have had. He was right, of course. I was not "of" the administration. I saw it as a game. I certainly never thought that my identity as a human being was in any way tied up with my success or failure as a senior officer of MIT. That is why it never occurred to me that "the system" might be sacrosanct. That was a major difference between John and me. I saw the system as just one more bureaucracy to outsmart, like trying to talk your way out of a parking ticket. You could play it any way you liked. John saw it the way a Vatican ecclesiastic views the papal hierarchy. You don't fool around with it. That is why John was provost and I would never be.

John's way of seeing things was brought home to me one day when I received a call from him informing me that someone under me in the great chain of command had overrun his budget by $50,000.

"I want you to call him in and deal with it," John said.

No sooner had I hung up the phone than John called again.

"Come to my office in forty-five minutes," he commanded. That was typical John Deutch. His view was that when something important needed to be done, he'd better do it himself. It was instructive that John considered this particular offense not a peccadillo but a felony.

When I arrived in John's office, the culprit and his immediate supervisor were there, all the principals in the relevant sector of the organization chart.

The spender defended himself by saying that he had indeed overspent his allotted dollars, but that it had been in a good cause. John replied with a short tutorial on how the system worked. It was an eye-opener for me. John pointed out that by overrunning the budget by $50,000, the culprit had unilaterally decided how a portion of the Institute's money would be spent. It was a violation of a fundamental principle of working within the system: no authority without responsibility. In short, spending that money was tantamount to spending someone else's money. It didn't matter whether the cause was a good one or not. It was a form of institutional misappropriation.

John turned to the violator's supervisor and said, "I'll cover you this year. But your budget for next year will be cut by $50,000."

That was it. The meeting was over. Shortly thereafter, the spender left the Institute to assume an even higher post somewhere else where, presumably, he could overspend with impunity.

The business of managing budgets troubled me. As a department head I was careful to stay within my budget's guidelines. But I always kept in the back of my mind what Cary Brown, a former distinguished head of the Economics Department, once told me. (People called him "the Silver Fox" because of his gray head of hair and his craftiness at playing the budget game.) He said, "A budget is not a record of how you spend your money. It is a theory of how you spend it."

In other words, budgets were like horoscopes. They were guesses about the future. I treated them with the circumspection that horoscopes deserve. That is, I treated them with multiple grains of salt. John must have detected that cavalier attitude in me. Doubtless he would have considered it a weakness. Even so, he didn't just take budgetary control away from me. Rather, he asked if I really wanted the power of the purse over the offices that reported to me or if I would rather he handle it. I told him I would like to think it over.

There was no question in my mind but that John could do in ten minutes what would take me ten hours. But being new to upper administration, I thought I'd better consider the full implications of his offer. This I did by making an appointment with the vice president and secretary to the Corporation, Constantine Simonides.

Constantine was the consummate senior administrator. He was the Institute's "fixer." Practically everything of importance at the Institute involved him in one way or another, either officially (MIT Medical, admissions, financial aid, career services, human resources, the news office, publications, government and community relations, the information center) or unofficially (everything else). Significantly, he was not a member of the MIT faculty. That was undoubtedly why a sizeable portion of the faculty was biased against him. They saw him as a handmaiden, someone completely at the service of his upper administration bosses. My own view was "What did you expect? That was his job." And from close up I thought he was superb at it. That was why I wanted to talk to him about John's question.

I settled into the black La-Z-Boy chair with the extending footrest that his large office so easily accommodated. The footrest flipped up at a touch of the wooden handle on the side, like a trainman's track-switcher. I inherited this chair when Constantine died. I kept it even though my office was a third the size of Constantine's. It seemed important not to let the chair die with him. When I retired, I passed it on to Robert Jaffe, a leading member of the Physics Department. Because Bob and I loved Constantine, we both thought it important that his chair be regularly sat in.

That afternoon was the first of many occasions when I lowered myself into the chair, arranged my legs just so and then pulled the handle that raised them up.

"John wants to know if I want to control the budgets of the people who report to me. What do you think?"

Constantine said, "At MIT if you want power, you have to control a budget. Otherwise, you are not a senior administrator."

"What are you?" I asked.

"A local stop on a railroad line," he said.

That was enough for me. I told John he should handle the budget. That, I think, is why John thought I was in the administration but not of it.

2   The Steps of Widener

I met Noam Chomsky in the spring of 1961, on the steps of Harvard's Widener Library. We went across the street to Nedick's for coffee. Widener is still there. Alas, Nedick's is not. I was there because Noam and Morris Halle were thinking about writing what, in my view, was a seminal work in twentieth-century linguistics, *The Sound Pattern of English*. For me that book is as important to linguistics as *Principia Mathematica* is to philosophy. Sadly, most linguists working today haven't even read it. By the same token most philosophers haven't read *Principia*. No matter. The book will rise again.

Why has it fallen by the wayside, at least for the moment? I can think of two reasons. The first is that it is simply too abstract for the taste of young phonologists. I once wrote Chomsky asking why he thought *Sound Pattern* had fallen on deaf ears. He wrote back, "A century ago the leading physicists dismissed the molecular theory of gases as a calculating system because there was no way to 'see' molecules. That continued with chemistry until my childhood. In the subjects dealing with humans, those drives are intensified by other factors." Noam didn't elaborate on those other factors. But here's one. There is a kind of intellectual parricide that haunts fields like linguistics, fields that are a cut above the soft sciences, like sociology and anthropology, but not quite at the hard science level, like physics, chemistry, and microbiology. In *The Brothers Karamazov* Alyosha asks, "Who among us would not wish to kill his own father?" That rings true of linguistics, I'm afraid—an adolescent science if there ever was one.

I was on Widener's steps that morning because Noam and Morris had a theory of how modern English phonology works. They wanted to know if it held for earlier stages of the language. My name came up. The reason was that after I graduated from George Washington University in 1956, I went to Oxford, England, on a Fulbright scholarship to study Old and Middle English philology at Merton College. I remain a member of the Fulbright Association to this day by way of expressing my gratitude though I don't think I've been to a single Fulbright event since my Oxford days. Even so, the program is in my heart.

My affection for it is partly the result of my experience with a rival program. My own university, George Washington, had nominated me for a Rhodes scholarship. I managed to make it to the interview stage. That was at Goucher College in Towson, Maryland. The interview is etched into my memory, partly because of the times. It was the height of the McCarthy era. The infamous hearings had not yet taken place, the ones in which Joseph Welch uttered his now iconic "Have you no sense of decency, sir?"

When I was called into the interview room, I found five men facing me. I remember only two of them. One was a Maryland judge by the name of Niles. The second was a Baltimore lawyer named Fisher. They must both be gone by now. The judge was running the show. I sat in a chair facing the panel. A large table separated us. The judge nodded to Fisher, who threw me softballs.

"What do you want to study at Oxford?"

"What's the point of studying a poem that is 700 years old?"

(Seamus Heaney's translation of *Beowulf* published in 2000 and Robert Zemeckis's 2007 movie, *Beowulf*, both testaments to the irrepressibility of the original epic, were fifty years in the future when Fisher put that question to me in 1956.)

At this point Judge Niles took over.

"What do you think of Senator McCarthy?" was his first question.

The question took me by surprise. I suppose I was still expecting softballs. Without thinking, I shot back, "He is a dangerous man."

Judge Niles raised his eyebrows. I took that as a sign that he wanted me to explain. So I did. I told the panel that a week before my interview McCarthy had pointed his finger at a black woman with a large family who worked at the Washington Navy Yard. Somehow her name had gotten onto his hit list. The newspapers were full of the story. She was dismissed without a hearing. She lost her job on the basis of the senator's accusation, cowardice on the part of the authorities, and an intimidated public that reacted to McCarthyism like a deer caught in headlights.

"I think this woman lost her job on the basis of hearsay," I said. "She wasn't given a hearing or a trial. That doesn't strike me as fair."

"In other words, young man," the judge said, "you don't think Communism is a threat to the United States."

"Am I being interviewed for a Rhodes scholarship or a job with the CIA?"

My outburst was followed by an awkward silence. The man named Fisher filled it with a few perfunctory questions. I was dismissed.

I walked out into the waiting room and looked around at the other candidates. Several of them were in military uniform. I should have put two and two together when I first came in. I sat down as I had been directed and waited. After an hour one of the interviewers came out, made his announcement, and thanked the rest of us. One of the uniformed candidates was asked to stay.

As I reached the door, I felt a hand on my shoulder. It was Fisher.

"If you don't get anything, give me a call," he said. He handed me his card.

I thanked him. The gesture took the sting out of the experience. I was grateful to him for that. As it happened, I did get something. To this day I regret not having called Mr. Fisher to tell him that. I had lost his card.

I worked hard at Oxford. My Fulbright was renewed for a second year. Who knew that I was setting myself up for a job at MIT? Life is like that. It rarely stretches ahead with the unbending single-mindedness of a Roman road. It is much more like a pinball in the grip of a dynamite flipper.

After Oxford, I enrolled in graduate studies in linguistics at Yale. In 1961, when I met Noam, I had finished my course work at Yale and was about to embark on writing my dissertation. At that point in my graduate career I was having second thoughts about linguistics. It seemed to me to be an exercise in cataloguing, rather than understanding, and while I didn't have the imagination to see how it might be done otherwise, I had enough sense to see that what I was learning at Yale wasn't going anywhere. I contemplated going to New York and trying my hand at publishing. That was when I got the call from MIT. What the hell, I thought. Cambridge isn't that far from New Haven.

Over coffee at Nedick's I listened to Noam explain what he and Morris were up to. All of a sudden we weren't talking about dead languages that survived in obscure texts like the *Ancrene Wisse*, a medieval rulebook for anchorite novices. Or the emendations in the latest edition of the Old English poem *The Exodus*. Now we were talking about how the mind works. This was a whole new ballgame. On the spot I decided to give up the year at University College London that I had been offered. Better to spend it at MIT and find out what these guys were doing. That was the smartest decision I ever made. It turned me from an amateur into a professional. It also taught me the importance of colleagues in academia. However good my work has been, it is twice as good as it would have been without the benefit of superb colleagues.

Wynton Marsalis once said that playing in a jazz band is like being in a marriage. The job of each musician is to make the others sound as good as possible. That's what scholarship in a healthy department is like. Each member of the department makes his or her colleagues as good as they can be. MIT certainly served me in that way.

Noam invited me to spend a year as a research affiliate at MIT. That September I met Morris. It was love at second sight. First sight had been more stressful. The year before I had gone down to New York for a meeting of the American Mathematical Society explicitly to hear Morris deliver a paper on historical phonology. This was supposed to be my field. The best philologists at Oxford, including J. R. R. Tolkien, had taught me. I was curious to see what all the MIT fuss was about. Morris's approach caught me completely off guard. I had never thought of language in that way. After the talk, people gathered around Morris asking questions. I pressed forward. I wanted to get into the act—that is, until I got close enough to hear what was going on. Most of the questioners circled around him like hornets whose nest had been bumped by a bear. Morris was unflinching, no more bothered by confrontation than an elephant by a flea. That is an attitude of mind I could never master. I'm a nonconfrontational kind of guy. I don't like fighting. Morris was made for it. He reacted to question after hostile question the way Wonder Woman and her magic bracelets react to a barrage of bullets. Each one just bounced off.

There was no way I was going to step into that buzz saw. I lurked at the periphery and listened. Then I went to lunch with a friend from Yale and tried to digest the meal and Morris. That afternoon I would never have guessed that Morris and I would become the closest of friends, a friendship that has lasted half a century.

The petri dish of our friendship was the Ninth International Congress of Linguists, held at MIT in August of 1962. It was the first time the congress had been held in the United States. Morris needed help organizing it, and he asked if I would pitch in. In the course of planning the congress, I told him to hire graduate students from the department to work as guides, ushers, gofers, whatever. I suggested he pay them $50 a day for the four days of the congress.

"Why pay them?" Morris asked. "They'll be glad to volunteer."

"If you pay them," I replied, "you can tell them what to do. If they don't, you can fire them."

Morris paid them. I told them what to do. He was Mr. Nice Guy. I was the other one. Several years later when Morris and one of the student workers were reminiscing about the congress, the student told Morris that working for me those four days was a real pain.

"Keyser was a son of a bitch," he said.

If Morris has told that story once over the years, he's told it a hundred times. I think it pleased him that he came off as the nice guy.

The Russians sent a contingent of three linguists. One of them, S. K. Shaumyan, ultimately ended up at Yale University. At one point during the four-day meeting they invited Morris and me to their rooms. They were living in one of the MIT dorms. They treated us to potato vodka, cheese, and black bread. I still remember the vodka. It was crystal clear, with a tiny worm that did somersaults in the bottle every time they poured us a shot. It was ice cold and the best vodka I've ever tasted.

The men accompanying Shaumyan spoke no English. Since I spoke no Russian, all communication was up to Morris, whose Russian was fluent. After we left, Morris said, "The two guys with Shaumyan aren't linguists. They didn't have a clue what I was talking about."

"I don't get it," I said. "If they're not linguists, who are they?"

"KGB agents," he answered. "They're keeping an eye on Shaumyan to make sure he doesn't defect."

My final year as a graduate student couldn't have been more schizophrenic. I was enrolled at Yale University. I spent all my time at MIT. Yale was the epitome of the old school of linguistics; MIT, the home of the young Turks. I would take all the courses I could during the week, learning what was wrong with the old way of doing things. On the weekends I wrote my dissertation the old way. I would send page after page to my advisor at Yale, Helge Kökeritz. He would make his comments. I would sheepishly incorporate the changes and send back more pages. It was as if I were living a double life. I felt like a deceiver, a husband who kept two wives. During the day I learned generative grammar. At night I did philology.

I didn't see any help for it. By this time I was convinced that what I was writing was nonsense. I was caught between a rock and a hard place. My thesis advisor, one of the world's great authorities on the pronunciation of William Shakespeare, railed against the MIT nonsense. I pressed on, writing on the weekends what I knew would please him. There was no way he would countenance my changing horses in midstream, at least with him as advisor. And there was no better advisor on the history of the English language.

Then there was a personal side of things. Helge came to see me as a disciple. In his case it mattered. He never married. He had been disappointed by his homeland, Sweden. Early in his career a distinguished professorship had gone to a rival, unfairly so in Helge's view, an appointment made on the basis of influence rather than achievement. Sweden broke his heart. So he left for America. By philological standards his career in America was star-studded. Being hired in the English Department at Yale was the pinnacle of that career. Years later when the Swedes recognized his achievements and made appropriate overtures, he went back, but always just for a visit, even when they offered him prestigious new positions. He couldn't turn his back on the country that gave him a job when Sweden didn't. But he couldn't turn his back on the country of his birth. The problem was that he only had one back. Had I told Helge that I had switched over to the enemy camp, his heart would have been broken. So I persisted in my dual life in the light during the week, in the dark on the weekends, literally; I worked in the basement.

Visiting another university while still a graduate student at Yale was not that unusual. After one had completed one's graduate classes, the dissertation could be written anywhere. After Noam's invitation, I had chosen to write mine while a visitor at MIT. Just before I left for MIT, Bernard Bloch, the legendary editor of *Language*—at the time the field's most prestigious journal—called me into his office. He wanted to know if I would like to do a book review for his journal. The book was *The Pronunciation of English in the Atlantic States*, a linguistic atlas that recorded the speech of several hundred speakers over an area reaching from Pennsylvania to South Carolina. Of course I would do the review. That was how one made one's way in academia. One published. Here I was, still a graduate student, and Bloch was offering me an opportunity to publish in the number one journal in the field. How could I not do it? I accepted with trepidation. I had never written a professional piece before, not even a book review. This would be my coming-out article. It didn't help that one of the atlas's authors, Hans Kurath, had been Bloch's mentor.

Bloch handed me a copy of the book, all 182 pages of it plus 180 full-page maps that recorded how people pronounced a large set of key words throughout the Atlantic States. It was a hefty volume and the weight of it brought home what it was I had agreed to do. I had no idea how I would do it. This was my trial by fire.

I knocked out a first draft of the review. I sat on it for a few days. I rewrote it, polishing it as best I could. Then I gave it to Morris.

He kept it for a day. Then he called me into his office.

"Keyser," he said. "This is a lousy piece of work."

"What's wrong with it?" I stammered.

"You're just trashing the book," he said.

"So?"

"That's too easy. If you don't like what the authors are doing, then show how to do it better yourself."

Morris was right. There was nothing creative about my review. I had written the academic version of a negative political ad. Reflecting on that moment some fifty years later, I realize that it was a watershed in my career as a linguist, in fact, the watershed. What it came down to was this: how do you handle criticism? Over the years I have encountered students and faculty who are unable to separate their work from themselves. A criticism of one is a criticism of the other. This is death to good work and also to good working relationships. I don't know what part of my character enabled me to say to myself: you can walk away and be pissed off and learn nothing, or you can listen to what this guy has to say and maybe learn something.

I studied the book in a completely different light. How could I demonstrate that there was a better way of doing this? I managed to find one. I took the data and showed that, looking at it from a different perspective, one could say some interesting things about how dialects differ along the Atlantic States and, in fact, in general. I rewrote my review and went back to Morris.

He kept it a day.

"Now you're talking," he said. "But you need to make the argument clearer."

I went back to Morris at least fifteen times. Each draft was better than the last. Finally, with the fifteenth draft he said, "Now it's ready to show to Chomsky."

I did just that. Noam read it, said he liked it, but wondered why I hadn't made a certain point about theoretical work in general. Another set of scales dropped from my eyes. In one simple comment Noam had raised the level of the review from good to important. I was flabbergasted. I was also grateful that I was at MIT.

I need to add a footnote to this account of how being among good colleagues is like playing in a jazz band. Bloch published the review no questions asked, even though it was hard on his mentor and his mentor's coauthor. I heard, though I have no direct evidence that this is true, that Bloch had been pressured not to publish the review. He was far too honest an editor not to resist such pressure if, indeed, it had been applied. In any event, thanks to the three of them, Bloch, Halle, and Chomsky, my reputation as a comer was made. I was never under any illusion that I could have gotten a start like that on my own.

3   The Making of a Department Head

No one is ever trained to be a department head. I don't know how this stacks up against comparable jobs in the private sector. Probably there are no comparable jobs. In academia you usually come to the position because you impress others as not being a threat. I suspect it is exactly the opposite in the corporate world. You get to the top (or near it) precisely because you are a threat.

There is another requirement. In academia you have to be good enough in your field so that you are not an embarrassment. Those are the sine qua non of a departmental headship. In other words, paraphrasing Polonius: neither a threat nor an embarrassment be.

There is always a measure of contempt mixed in with whatever respect you may command. What scholar in his or her right mind would ever want to take time away from the high calling of scholarship to deal with the mundane details of running a department? The Salvation Army has its three S's: Soap, Soup, and Salvation. Individual faculty members have theirs: Salary, Space, and a Secretary. (With the advent of computers, the last S disappeared.) Each member of the department you are about to head assesses you in terms of the question: is he/she good for me? If you score high enough, you get the nod. Obviously, the person who is looking for someone who is best for him will only be satisfied with himself. That is why department heads are always everyone's second choice.

There are, of course, toughening experiences so that if one day you do end up running a department, you find that unbeknownst to yourself, events have been grooming you all along. One such experience happened when I was starting out as an assistant professor at Brandeis University. I couldn't have come at a worse time. The year I joined the faculty was 1965, just two years after the United States had entered the war in Vietnam. Those Brandeis years were tumultuous, beginning with crescendoing anti–Vietnam War activities on campus and off and culminating in the black student takeover of Ford and Sydeman Halls in January 1969.

The black students occupied the building to gain attention and support for ten innocuous demands: establishment of an African Studies Department, a black-student-designed student center, more black faculty, and so on. Most of them were ultimately granted. The Brandeis president at the time was Morris Abram. He was inaugurated in October 1968, just three months before the takeover. This was his first major crisis.

When the students took over the halls, the faculty, myself included, were thrown into a tizzy. Our sympathies were with the students. Our loyalties were with the university. We were constantly being whiplashed between the two, astonished that our university suddenly had become the sole province of a band of activist students on the one hand and administrators on the other. The faculty was, in a single night, marginalized.

Only we didn't realize it at the time.

I think of the cartoon where the swordsman swipes at his cartoon adversary. The adversary says, "You missed." The swordsman says, "Wait 'til you try to turn your head."

All the while the theatrics of takeover were, well, taking over, I had thought we faculty members were relevant to the crisis. That was a fundamental mistake. I found that out one evening when I was called upon to give an account of a meeting between the black students and a small group of colleagues. The meeting took place inside Ford Hall itself. My colleagues and I thought we were working out some kind of negotiated settlement. When we reached the hall, the students told us to climb through a window adjacent to the main entrance. Ostensibly, the students had locked the front door against a police rush. Afterward, I realized that our awkward and unceremonious entrance had another, far more symbolic meaning. The students could easily have opened the door, let us slip in, and locked it behind us. They were far more skilled in psyops than we were. They made us work to get in. For me negotiating the window entry was awkward. I must have looked foolish, straining to get one leg over the sill and then the other. Athletic I am not. The entry scenario was a setup, of course, a subtle way of putting us, the faculty negotiators, in our places. It was the occupiers' way of telling us who was in charge.

After a wait of several minutes, a number of black student leaders joined us. We talked about how to present their demands to the president and the faculty, how we might bring about an equitable resolution. I took it all very seriously. That night I dutifully delivered a summary to an audience in Mailman Hall, the student center where such general meetings usually took place. Students were sitting on the floors, on tables, on the stairs with their legs dangling between the balusters. The atmosphere was almost giddy, conspiratorially giddy, what with everyone feeling as if they were in on the ground floor. Brandeis history was being made. Blows were being struck against discrimination. Injustice was being righted. We were all a little drunk on the wine of at last doing something meaningful. Almost all of us.

During my segment of the evening, someone interrupted me. Even though it was more than forty years ago, I could still pick him out of a lineup. He wore military fatigues that were stiff from being unwashed. He had a thick Rip Van Winkle beard and hair that streamed down around his ears and neck. He was heavy-lidded and sat cross-legged, smoking a cigarette. He was not a student. Nor was he a faculty member or a Brandeis administrator. He was one of the many mysterious characters who showed up at these kinds of meetings in those kinds of times. Someone told me he was an ex-marine.

At a pause in my report he broke into the discussion. "You want to be part of the action? Take over another building. Otherwise, it's all bullshit."

It turns out he couldn't have been more right. While my colleagues and I were engaged in saving the university, the leader of the takeover and the president of Brandeis were riding around Waltham at midnight in a black limousine. That was how the crisis was settled, just ten days after it started.

That was my first lesson in academic politics. When there is a crisis, the administration and the building occupiers hold all the cards. The faculty are merely bystanders. If they think otherwise, just wait until they try to turn their heads.

Those times couldn't have been more insane. That was not surprising. Insanity on the part of a government that went to war in Vietnam bred insanity at home. There were many national manifestations of it, most notably the killings at Kent State. I'll never forget hearing a bone-chilling comment from a father whose child was a student at Kent State: that if it had been his child on that hill, he would have deserved to be shot. Shades of Dostoevsky.

I experienced a touch of the insanity that was rampant in the country within the precincts of Brandeis itself. In February 1970, as part of a government program designed to enroll ex-convicts, Brandeis admitted a young man named Stanley Bond. This was the Stanley Bond who robbed a bank in Brighton, Massachusetts, in September of the same year he enrolled at Brandeis. The proceeds from the robbery were going to help fund the revolution. In that robbery a police officer, Walter Schroeder, was shot in the back and killed. Bond and two accomplices were captured almost immediately. Two women went into hiding. They were Susan Saxe and Katherine Anne Powers. Saxe was arrested in Philadelphia in 1975 and spent eight years in prison. Powers was on the run for twenty-three years. In 1993 she turned herself in.

I mention all of this because one day in the spring of 1970 the dean of the college called me into his office.

"Do you know a student named Stanley Bond?" he asked.

"No," I replied.

"Well, he knows you."

"So?"

"If he comes into your office and asks you for anything—and I mean anything—just tell him yes."

"Why?" I asked.

"Because he carries a gun," the dean said.

I was speechless. This was way beyond my comfort zone.

"A gun?" I echoed.

"He's part of our ex-convict program. He just enrolled."

"But a gun? Why does he carry a gun?"

"So do I," said the dean as if that somehow explained everything.

He gestured toward the top drawer of his massive decanal desk.

"I keep it handy when he comes to see me. Just in case."

Just in case of what? I was dumbfounded. I left his office in a fog. For the next week I went through the motions of meeting classes, giving lectures, and grading papers. Everything seemed to be in slow motion. During office hours, whenever an unfamiliar student came to my office door, my heart stopped. After a week I couldn't bear it any longer. These were not the working conditions I had hired onto. I decided I would stay home until Stanley Bond and his gun were removed from campus. Brandeis would have to choose between an armed student ex-convict and me.

The dean typically presided over faculty meetings. I decided to wait outside the meeting. I would buttonhole him as he left. An entourage of faculty wanting this or that always surrounded him. He glided through the doors of the meeting hall like a rock star.

"I have to talk to you about Stanley Bond," I yelled, loud enough for him to hear.

"What about him?" The dean stopped suddenly, extracted himself from the hangers-on, and came over to where I was standing.

"You warned me about him. You said he knew me. I was supposed to give him whatever he asked for when he came to see me. You told me he carried a gun."

The dean stood there looking at me as if I were speaking a foreign language.

"I can't teach under these conditions," I started to say. I was about to launch into a protracted argument about why it was unreasonable to expect a faculty member to operate in an environment in which a student was carrying a gun with a bullet that might have his initials on it.

The dean didn't let me finish. "I remember now. I guess I forgot to tell you. You're not the right faculty member. It was somebody else."

That was the second time I was stunned into silence by a conversation with this dean. He simply turned away, picked up his entourage like a mother hen gathering her chicks and disappeared out the door.

Five months later Bond left Brandeis to rob the Brighton branch of the State Street Bank and Trust Company. Two years later he blew himself up in prison making a bomb that he was going to use to escape.

These two experiences—the Ford Hall takeover and Stanley Bond—taught me a very important lesson about academia, one that stood me in excellent stead when I became a department head. It was that life inside the academy was not insulated from the insanity that swirled outside its ivory towers. The only thing different was the stakes. Outside the stakes were measured in terms of property. Inside the stakes were measured in terms of power or rather the absence of it. As an academic friend of mine once put it: in the academy powerlessness corrupts; absolute powerlessness corrupts absolutely. I don't think "corrupts" is the right word. I would substitute another: powerlessness deranges; absolute powerlessness deranges absolutely.

A consequence of my experience at Brandeis was, in a word, distance. I somehow came out of all that with an ability to keep the people that I had to deal with at arm's length. It was a hard thing to do. Psychiatrists, I'm told, take courses in learning how not to become involved in the lives of their patients. I learned how not to become involved in the trials of the people I had to deal with. The way I did this was to picture administration as a game, one that I would either win or lose. But one in which nothing much was at stake.

To the extent that I was a good administrator, I think it was because my Brandeis experience taught me not to take anything that happened in academia seriously, except, of course, the pursuit of knowledge.

4   The Life of a Department Head

In the spring of 1977 MIT offered me the headship of the newly created Department of Linguistics and Philosophy. Morris Halle, my mentor and friend, called to give me the news.

"I can't tell you why you should take the job, but I can tell you why you shouldn't."

"Which is?" I asked.

"You have it made where you are."

Morris was a cunning man. The last thing in the world I wanted was to "have it made."

I took the job at MIT.

The department that I was leaving, the Linguistics Department at the University of Massachusetts at Amherst, was in large part the reason MIT offered me the job. I had gone to UMass from Brandeis five years earlier. At the time the UMass department was ranked twenty-sixth in the nation. When I left, it was in the top ten. My job had been to make that difference.

Doing it was sheer hell. If I had known how hard it was going to be, I don't think I would have accepted the job. From the outside it might appear that a department head is a high-level paper pusher, someone who arranges teaching schedules, prepares promotion cases, assigns pay raises at the end of the year, does a little teaching, and takes three months off. That couldn't be farther from the truth.

In academia everything depends on personnel. If you want to have the best department, you have to hire the best faculty. That also often means you have to fire people. When Neil Sedaka wrote "Breaking Up Is Hard to Do," he wasn't just writing a love song.

Once you've got the best faculty, you have to be prepared to offer them the best students. It's a finely balanced system. Each group has to be worthy of the other if the system is to run smoothly. The forces at work to keep a system from changing are extraordinarily conservative. They include the social relationships that have been built between the faculty, between the students, and, sometimes uncomfortably, between the faculty and the students. For an outsider to come in and attempt to alter those lines of social force is threatening. Some will take up arms against change using whatever weapons are at hand. In my case one of those taking up arms was an ex-student. His weapon was the judicial system.

One of my first duties as a new department head at the University of Massachusetts was to decide on new admissions to the graduate program. One student in particular came to my attention. He had already been a student in the department but had taken the year off. He had neglected to pay a $10 registration fee. Had he paid the fee, he would have retained his place in the department. But since he hadn't, he was forced to reapply. The admissions committee reviewed his application and concluded that the quality of work he was producing wasn't commensurate with the time already spent in the program. The committee recommended against readmission. I agreed. Since I was head of the department, the student took me to court along with the dean of the School of Humanities, the dean of the Graduate School, and, as I recall, the chancellor as well.

This was a hard first lesson to learn as a department head. What you do in the course of your ordinary duties can be actionable. In retrospect I shouldn't have been surprised. But also in retrospect it was like carrying a backpack filled with bricks. I was trying to make the department a better place. I was sued in the process.

A pro bono group of lawyers affiliated with Harvard Law School took the student's case. Something close to ten years went by before I was called into the courtroom. I had already moved from the University of Massachusetts to MIT. What that meant for me was ten years of buried anxiety. Most of the time I was able to put the case out of my mind. But there were times when I couldn't. What would happen if the student were to win? Would I be personally liable? Would I lose my home? Would I have to forfeit a significant portion of my income to pay compensatory damages? Was all this worth it just to raise a department from twenty-sixth place to the top ten—a department I was no longer affiliated with? This was the first time I wondered whether the game was worth the candle. It wouldn't be the last. I had made a judgment about the academic qualifications of a student. A lawyer was ready to argue that I had acted unjustly. In the course of doing what I saw as my job, I suddenly found myself embroiled in what could be—depending on the outcome—extremely debilitating litigation. Now I knew how surgeons must feel. Trying to help others, like cigarette smoking, can be harmful to your health.

I remember the courtroom scene, especially. I was extremely nervous. I hadn't met with the lawyers at the University of Massachusetts for several years. I had, by that time, been at MIT for three years. I felt as if I were going it alone.

Presiding over the trial was David Nelson, a highly respected Federal District Court judge, who was the first African American appointed to the federal judiciary in Massachusetts. The examination that follows is my recollection of that day. I couldn't test its accuracy against the court records because, oddly enough, when I inspected those records, my testimony was missing. Everything else seemed to be there. I write this exchange in full knowledge of the truism that the past is less a record of what happened than a theory of what happened.

Lawyer: Did you seek any outside advice in judging the plaintiff's work?

Me: No.

Lawyer: Why not?

Me: I didn't think it was necessary.

Lawyer: You mean you took it upon yourself to judge the work yourself?

Me: Yes.

Lawyer: Isn't that presumptuous?

Me: No.

Lawyer: Are you in the habit of making such judgments?

Me: Yes.

Lawyer: Why is that?

Me: That's my job.

At some point in the proceedings the counsel for the plaintiff called a faculty member at another university to the stand. I was surprised to see him in the courtroom and even more surprised when I realized he was testifying as an expert witness on behalf of the plaintiff. He told the court that in his opinion the graduate student had been harmed by my decision not to readmit him. He had been stigmatized by the action. Any sister institution would surely "question" such an applicant. Thank goodness the judge disagreed, noting that my colleague had testified that "he had no personal experience with such a case, nor had he ever heard such a case reported by other colleagues." The judge went on to say that the plaintiff had failed to supply any evidence to support the stigmatization complaint other than "the speculation of himself" and of my colleague.

When he had finished testifying, my colleague stopped to talk to me on his way out of the courtroom. He said he was sorry but he saw testifying as a duty. I never understood that. I didn't see being an expert witness for one side or the other as anyone's duty. And in any event, why would a teacher want to participate in a case that, if it went for the plaintiff, would go against the right of a faculty member to judge a student?

I didn't realize it at the time, but it is an established principle of law that university officials are given a great deal of latitude when it comes to making judgments about their students or fellow colleagues. Even had I known that at the time, I doubt it would have helped lower my fret level. I tend to expect the worst, especially when it is about me. I certainly did in this case. I came out of that courtroom not knowing whether I had dodged a bullet or not. Apparently I had.

That famous line from *The Tempest*, "What's past is prologue," is carved outside the National Archives in Washington, where it stands as a warning to the nation not to sink into ignorance. It could equally well serve as the moral of my court case. I was soon to learn that even at MIT the hardest part of the job was removing people from the community. Once someone was admitted, getting him or her out was rather like a divorce. It was extremely hard to make it happen, and almost impossible to do without pain.

My first year on the job, in the spring of 1978, I discovered that one of our graduate students had not received a grade in eleven subjects. Not receiving a grade generally meant that the student owed a faculty member a term paper, in this case eleven papers. The student was also receiving financial support. There was the rub. Students who received departmental funding had to be "in good standing." For the department, "good standing" meant no more than three incompletes. Eleven incompletes was not in good standing times four!

How can this sort of thing happen? Well, not to put too fine a point on it, because faculty members let it happen. A faculty member knows the student is good, understands the work, and is creative. The faculty member wants to be supportive. So when the student asks for an incomplete, the faculty member gives it. There it ends. There's no bookkeeping system that automatically kicks in when three incompletes have been amassed. The department head *is* the bookkeeper. I don't write this with a holier-than-thou attitude. There is a department head in the country now who still owes me a paper.

With respect to the eleven incompletes, I had no recourse. Either I had to attest falsely that a student was in good standing or funds had to be denied, a move tantamount to forcing the student out of the department.

The way things worked at the Institute, I could not unilaterally take such action. I had to submit the case to a higher authority, the Committee on Graduate School Policy. I wanted the department to rule on the matter. My colleagues enjoyed department meetings as much as a cat enjoys a bath. "You do it," they said. So, without calling a department meeting, I ruled on the matter and wrote a letter to the committee requesting that the student not be readmitted to the department.

The committee granted my request. I so informed the student. The next day all hell broke loose. Twenty graduate students filed into my office, demanding to know why I had done what I had done.

"Ask the student," I said.

"We want to hear from you," the spokesman replied.

"I can't talk about it," I said. "It would be a breach of confidentiality. If the student wants to talk about it, that's fine with me. I can't."

This is not an unusual MIT scenario. Someone—a student, a staff member, a faculty member—feels put upon for some reason or other: say, denial of funding, wrongful termination of employment, withholding of tenure. That person goes public, claiming unfair treatment. Confidentiality prevents the administration from making the details public. A public fight follows, only one of the pugilists in the fray has his hands tied behind his back. This usually works itself out with either the public losing interest or the matter going to court, where confidentiality is no longer an issue. In my case what happened was that the student representatives demanded that there be a faculty meeting to discuss the matter. I agreed.

Whenever students feel strongly about an issue, the faculty's reticence to meet is overcome. This reaction on the part of the faculty is a complicated one. In part it derives from a sense of guilt at the power differential between faculty members and their students. Most faculty members are uncomfortable with that power. They bend over backward to pretend it isn't there. But it always is. Faculty members have to make a judgment about how well a student is doing. There are no two ways about it. Not to perform that judgment fairly and accurately is a dereliction of duty. These boundaries can never be erased. When they are, the faculty member becomes some kind of fellow traveler, a pal, not a student and not a teacher—neither flesh, fish, nor good red herring.

When the faculty meeting took place, I explained the situation. Someone suggested that we overlook the rules in this case. The student, this faculty member argued, was obviously smart, made important contributions in class, could easily write a dissertation. So what was the point of putting an end to the student's career? I took the position that if I was to administer the rules, then I had to administer them consistently. I offered the faculty a compromise: change the rule and I'll change my decision. The faculty thought the rule was a good one. It remained unchanged. So did my decision. In the end the student made up the incompletes, was readmitted, and became a contributing member of the field. So what was all the fuss about? I think it was about a student being held accountable for his actions and a faculty not wanting to be the accountant.

Recently one of the students who marched into my office, now a successful member of an important Internet corporation, visited with me and recalled the "sit-in."

"You were right," the former student said. "We shouldn't have blamed you."

I was glad that the student had seen it from my point of view, even if it took thirty years for the message to get back to me. But I hadn't beaten myself up about it. My friend Morris had taught me early on that whenever a tricky situation arose, the best thing to do was to figure out what the principle was. Once you understood that, it was duck soup to figure out what to do. In this case the principle was easy: rules are for everyone. I wasn't happy about being called the departmental tyrant, but the principle did double duty as a shield.

II   et Mania

5   To Be or Not to Be a University

In 1985 MIT's new provost, John Deutch, asked me to become associate provost for educational programs and policy. I had been department head for seven years and the idea of a new job was appealing. I had been deeply influenced by Leonard Woolf's five-volume autobiography. In one of the volumes (I think it was *Growing: An Autobiography of the Years 1904 to 1911*), he said that he had made it a point to change professions every seven years. It was how he stayed mentally young. That seemed like a good idea to me. After seven years I'd pretty much gotten the hang of being department head. The future offered more of the same. Like Monty Python, it was time for something completely different. I accepted the job.

Associate provost for educational programs and policy was a new position of John's own design, triggered, I suspect, by an MIT reappraisal of the role of the humanities in a curriculum strongly biased toward science and engineering. When John stepped down as provost in 1990, he was interviewed by the student newspaper and had this to say:

Q: What do you think was your greatest success during your time as provost?

A: I don't know that I would mark any one thing as my greatest success. I believe that when I became provost, Paul Gray and

I spoke about having the Institute pay more attention to undergraduate education, and that the appointment of Jay Keyser as Associate Provost, the establishment of the Dean for Undergraduate Education, the establishment of the Committee on Undergraduate Education, and the development of an entire series of discussions and committees to review undergraduate education, have in my view been a very necessary and productive rebalancing of the attention of MIT. . . . That, I think, has been the single most important hallmark of the last five years that I've been involved in.

John's recap of his greatest success at MIT didn't quite jibe with my own experience. Here I was, hired to focus on undergraduate education. Instead I found myself caught up in a maelstrom of pornography, harassment, and antiapartheid protests. That isn't to say that John didn't achieve the rebalancing he was looking for. The Committee on Undergraduate Programs that John created was here to stay. (It is still going strong.) But I didn't chair it. That fell to dean Margaret MacVicar, the founder of one of MIT's most successful undergraduate programs, UROP (Undergraduate Research Opportunities Program). This program makes it possible for undergraduates to work alongside faculty engaged in cutting-edge research. The genius of UROP is that it treats MIT undergraduates as if they are junior colleagues. For a significant number of them, taking part in UROP is their signature experience at the Institute. It was perfectly natural that Margaret would become the point guard for undergraduate educational reform. Tragically, just fifteen months after John stepped down as provost, Margaret died of cancer. Who knows what she might have been able to do for undergraduate education at the Institute had she lived?

Probably not very much. If I felt like a fish that had found its way to the sea, Margaret was more like a salmon doomed to swim upstream. John Deutch believed that someone ought to keep an overseeing eye on the undergraduate curriculum. What better choice than Margaret MacVicar, the mother of the brilliant UROP program? He made her the first dean for undergraduate education and put her at the head of the first Committee on Undergraduate Programs. Her portfolio included, among other things, reshaping the undergraduate curriculum to meet her own vision of an MIT education. The problem was that the curriculum was not in her hands. It was in the hands of the academic deans. They were the ones who made the decisions about who would teach what and when. It was part and parcel of the MIT ethos to keep curriculum decisions close to those who teach it. Consequently, a good portion of Margaret's decanal career was spent trying to wrest some of that power away from the deans. And that wasn't going to happen. In academia as everywhere else—with the exception of the king of Bhutan—no one with power gives it up. Margaret's struggle was compounded by an even deeper struggle at the Institute.

MIT has always had trouble knowing how best to describe itself. James R. Killian, the tenth president, gave by far the most famous description in his April 2, 1949, inaugural address when he said that MIT was "a special type of educational institution which can be defined as a university polarized around science, engineering, and the arts. We might call it a university limited in its objectives but unlimited in the breadth and the thoroughness with which it pursues these objectives." So we were "limited"— in other words, a university but not a real one. I always thought Killian protested too much. We were what we were. Shortly after I was appointed associate provost, I received a telephone call from the New York Times. The reporter wanted to know what I thought about MIT's self-induced reappraisal of the role of the humanities in its curriculum. I was thunderstruck. The New York Times was calling moi. Here I was, not three months into the job and my opinion was being sought. That was the problem. I gave

them my opinion. Here is a snippet from the beginning of an
article dated September 23, 1985:

It would be incorrect to say that M.I.T., an institution long pre-eminent
in the teaching of science and engineering, is going soft. Nor is it true,
said Samuel J. Keyser, the new associate provost for educational programs and policy, that the 9,400-student institute aspires to become a
center of universal knowledge. "M.I.T. is not a university," Dr. Keyser
insisted.

A day after the article appeared, I got an angry note from a former provost telling me that I was talking nonsense when I said
MIT is not a university, that I should be careful what I said. It
didn't help that I found a quote that agreed with me from a
past Institute president. I sent it along to support my view. The
silence at the other end of the note was deafening.

This business of whether MIT is a university or not was a
touchy one ever since the government started pouring money
into it at the beginning of World War II. That war wrought a
profound change, not only at MIT but at institutions of higher
learning all over the world, a change that shifted focus from
teaching to research. The proper balance between the two has
been a matter of ongoing concern for institutions of higher
learning ever since. MIT's history is not unique so much as it is
illustrative.

MIT received its founding charter from the Commonwealth
of Massachusetts on April 10, 1861, just two days before the start
of the Civil War. It began as a technical school. Well before 1930
it had developed into the nation's most respected engineering school. Anyone with the slightest interest in the humanities wouldn't touch it with a ten-foot slide rule. In 1930 Karl
Taylor Compton became president. He made it his mission to
raise MIT's intellectual profile. He began by hiring world-class
physicists and mathematicians. By the time of World War II
it approached in science what it had achieved in engineering.

Compton's program was so successful that today MIT's engineering faculty can teach foundational courses in physics and vice versa. I have personally sat in on conversations between engineers and physicists where the topic was quantum mechanics and if you had to guess which was the physicist and which the engineer, you would do best to flip a coin.

The last major change to the school structure of MIT came in 1952 when James R. Killian, the man who described MIT as a "limited university," created the School of Humanities, Arts, and Social Sciences. This gave MIT the patina of an unlimited university. Under the new school's umbrella disciplines like history, English literature, philosophy, political science, economics, and, in 1965, linguistics, came in out of the rain.

The changing complexion of the school caught some of the administration by surprise. When it was first announced in the *New York Times* that MIT's Linguistics Department had been voted number one in some poll or other, Howard Johnson, MIT's twelfth president, was midair between Boston and New York. A companion handed him the *New York Times* with the news.

Howard is reported to have said, "I didn't know we had a Linguistics Department." I once asked Howard if that was a true story. He said he didn't remember saying it, but he gave me the impression that he might well have.

Even though Linguistics was number one in the country—and the world for that matter, due largely to the presence of Noam Chomsky on its faculty—it has never been a separate department. At one point it was a section of Foreign Languages and Literatures. Then it became, for alphabetical reasons, the first conjunct in the newly formed Department of Linguistics and Philosophy, the one that I was hired to head in 1977. The engine of that metamorphosis was insecurity.

The previous year the Humanities Department was being scrutinized by the Institute in one of its cyclic efforts to bring humanities up to the level of science and engineering. It was an umbrella department and there was talk of eliminating some of its ribs. Philosophy was one. The linguists didn't want that to happen, largely because there were a number of first-rate philosophers in the section. MIT would be diminished without them. So Morris Halle went to the dean of the School of Humanities, Arts, and Social Sciences, Harry Hanham, and suggested a joint department made up of linguistics and philosophy. The dean was interested. There was a catch. Morris said it would need a department head. He was not about to head it up. That's where I came in. In the end it was a win-win situation. The philosophers got out from under whatever ax might be about to fall on them. Morris got out from under any administrative responsibility, the Institute effected economies by having two sections run by a single support staff, and I, a fish out of water, got to swim in the sea.

The effort to improve the humanities wasn't hindered by this defection. In fact, today the humanities at MIT are incredibly strong, with world-class historians, musicians, composers, playwrights, novelists, and poets, at least three Pulitzer Prize winners among them. Surely, this is enough to make MIT a university.

So when did MIT become the university that everyone considers it today? In a Voice of America broadcast (January 21, 1964) Julius Stratton, MIT's eleventh president, was asked to address the question "how [MIT] has come to assume in recent years the character of a modern university." Why would anyone think that was an interesting question? Stratton clearly did. He argued that MIT's passage into university-hood began in the 1930s when American institutions of higher learning began to emulate the strong emphasis on basic scientific research that had characterized European centers of higher learning such as those in Berlin, Copenhagen, Göttingen, Paris, and Zurich. That was step 1. Step 2 was taken as a result of World War II. Basic science found itself having to take into consideration the environment in which science was practiced. That meant taking an interest in the social sciences, economics, political science, even management. And that led to step 3, the founding of a School of Humanities, Arts, and Social Sciences. Voilà! MIT was a university. Even so, Stratton was ambivalent about the name: "It is highly unlikely that the Massachusetts Institute of Technology will ever abandon a name that has earned such respect through the years. Yet I hope that you will associate with this name the interests, the liberal outlook, and the character of a modern university."

I think of Stratton's account as the rose-by-any-other-name theory. I personally favor a different account, one proposed by Joel Moses. I call it the testimonial theory. I take the term from *The Wizard of Oz*. When the Tin Man claimed that he didn't have a heart, the Wizard gave him a testimonial thanking him for his many acts of kindness. He had had a heart all along.

Like the Tin Man, MIT-qua-university needed a testimonial. That testimonial was awarded in November 1983, thirty-one years after the creation of the School of Humanities, Arts, and Social Sciences. *U.S. News and World Report* published its America's Best Colleges rankings for the first time. MIT ranked tenth in a tie with Dartmouth in the category "National Universities." That was MIT's testimonial. The point is, it's no good calling yourself a university any more than it is calling yourself a gentleman. It's up to others to do that for you.

A few years after my appointment as associate provost I learned that a previous MIT president and his irate ex-provost had urged John not to name me to the position. The reason for their opposition was that I had once served on a committee that recommended ending a program the provost and his president had been instrumental in starting. It was their baby. The committee I served on found that the program had internal

leadership problems. Outside funding had dried up. It was cost-
ing the provost's office $300,000 a year. To me (and to the other
three committee members I served with) it seemed like a no-
brainer. It never occurred to me to consider the reactions of the
program's founding fathers, who were long gone from the daily
flow of Institute affairs.

The truth was that I had been caught up in a sea change at
MIT. Jerry Wiesner, the thirteenth president of MIT, had contributed mightily to the growth of humanities at the Institute,
spending great gobs of money to build up that side of the house.
Little did I realize that my serving on that committee was a sign
that the spending spree had to stop. That was my function,
although I had no idea at the time that that was what I was
doing.

This experience taught me two lessons, both of which are relevant not only to MIT but to academia in general. The first was
that administrators think of the programs they have initiated
the way artists think of their paintings. They are sacrosanct. Egos
are attached to programs like strings on a puppet.

The second lesson is that while MIT, a great innovator, is very
good at starting things, it is miserable at stopping them. The program I voted into oblivion was an example. The act of stopping
it left permanent scars that only the grave was able to obliterate.
As the song says, "Breaking up is hard to do."

I think the reason isn't too hard to fathom. The faculty uproar
so often heard at the closing of a department can be paraphrased
as "Who's running this place? You or us?" The faculty has always
been under the useful illusion that it runs things. When the
administration shuts something down, it threatens that view.
It spells out in no uncertain terms: faculty are employees; the
administration is boss. Yet at MIT and, I suspect, at most other
institutions of higher learning, the truth is that no matter what

the real lines of power are, the faculty had better be kept happy or it will pick up its marbles and look for another game.

It's a tricky business. Best to let the faculty think it is running things. But the administration had better do a good job behind the scenes. If it screws up, confrontation is inevitable, usually on the floor of a faculty meeting—the president of the Institute is ex-officio president of the faculty and typically chairs its meetings—and the truth about where the power lies and where the fault lines are is revealed. That makes both parties uncomfortable. Think of the scene at the end of *The Wizard of Oz* where Toto pulls back the curtain to reveal Frank Morgan pulling the levers that make the Wizard roar. That's what it's like at a faculty meeting when the administration is called to task. Nobody knows where to look.

MIT has managed this tricky situation by blurring the line between administration and faculty as much as possible. One of the ways of fuzzying the line is through the presidency. For almost half a century—right up until May 15, 1991, when MIT inaugurated its fifteenth president, Charles M. Vest—every president of MIT had come from within the Institute. Even Chuck became president after an MIT insider had turned the post down. That was Phil Sharp. His nomination was announced in the MIT *Tech* on February 15, 1990, under the headline "Phillip Sharp Next President." One week later, on February 21, the headline read "Sharp Declines Presidency." Sharp said that when the time actually came to say, "I do," he couldn't get the words out of his mouth. To marry the Institute, he would have had to divorce science, and when it came to science, Sharp was a strict Catholic. He put it this way: "As I began to disband my research group and to plan a future without active participation with my peers in research and teaching, I was unprepared for the acute sense of loss I experienced. I assure you that the difficult and awkward decision to withdraw my nomination was made on this personal basis." Shortly thereafter a reconvened selection committee turned outside for the first time in half a century.

This was an important moment for the Institute. An outsider threatened the view that the administration is just the faculty in suits. For a period of five years between 1990 and 1995, MIT went through a kind of foreign body reaction, unsure whether to accept or reject the new president. Part of the reason was that Chuck had not risen through the MIT ranks like his predecessor, Paul Gray. Paul had run the gamut from undergraduate to graduate to instructor to assistant professor to associate professor to professor. He was associate dean for student affairs, associate provost, dean of the School of Engineering, and, finally, chancellor before becoming the fourteenth president of MIT. Paul is what is known at MIT as a lifer. He had been through the MIT mill. Chuck was a complete outsider. To acknowledge the tie between faculty and administration, Chuck asked for and was given a faculty appointment in the Mechanical Engineering Department. A formal case was put together just as it would have been for any faculty member. Would the case have made it through had Chuck not been president? Who knows? It didn't matter. For Chuck this was a matter of principle; a president should be a member of the faculty. Chuck was very much in the spirit of MIT. Even so, this didn't make up for the inside-track route, as everyone knew, most of all Chuck himself.

From the very beginning of his tenure as president, Chuck paid attention not to the internal affairs of the Institute but to its external affairs. This was partly due to the wall that existed between him, the outsider, and the faculty, the insiders. But it was partly due to Chuck's own preference. He viewed the stewardship of MIT as a national calling. He believed that education in the United States was being dissed by pop culture. He believed it was critical to turn that around. So he was happy to look outward. The faculty was happy to have him do so.

Chuck managed to do the impossible. He became an honorary insider. It took an extraordinary event to make that happen. That was the so-called Overlap case. Chuck decided to fight a United States Department of Justice lawsuit alleging that MIT and its Ivy League sisters were in violation of the Sherman Antitrust Act. Each year the Overlap Group compared the ability of families to pay for the education they were seeking for their children at their respective institutions. This helped to determine how much financial aid each institution was prepared to offer incoming students. The government called it price-fixing. When the government claimed violation of the antitrust laws, all the other institutions, including Harvard, caved. The president of Harvard at the time, Neil Rudenstine, said publicly that the lawsuit wasn't worth the effort—that it was, in effect, "small potatoes."

Chuck thought otherwise. He decided that setting need-based levels of support was not a "commercial" act, but a charitable one. It was a way of making sure that the Ivy Leaguers didn't compete with one another for the best students the way baseball teams compete for players. Setting need-based levels of support made the money go farther and allowed for the support of more students. In the end MIT won. Win or lose, the faculty was proud that MIT had taken a principled position. It was especially proud of having done so alone. Chuck Vest suddenly became an insider. When he finally stepped down from the presidency after fourteen years in office, the outpouring of affection for him was genuine.

The real importance of Chuck's stand becomes clear when you realize that taking the matter to court was a wholly symbolic act. The reason is that all the other schools with which MIT traditionally set need levels had agreed not to challenge the government. They signed consent agreements with the Department of Justice. That left MIT with no one else at the table. MIT was like Joseph Haydn at the end of the *Farewell* Symphony. No one was left to play the music. From a practical point of view Chuck didn't have to sue. Nevertheless he did. It was the principle of the thing. In "Moving On," his last report as president of MIT, Chuck described that moment this way:

As a neophyte president, I was lobbied kindly but firmly by more experienced fellow presidents I greatly admired not to challenge the Justice Department. The stakes, and potential treble damages, they said, were too high to risk in a court battle.

Then the moment came—I was on the phone in my study talking with Thane Scott, a fine young attorney, and Constantine Simonides, a remarkable MIT administrator and a spiritual force in the Institute. They explained that time had run out. I had to tell them whether to sign a consent decree or go to court.

After a long pause, I said, "We are going to court."

The effect on the faculty and the administration of Chuck's decision to "push back"—as Constantine would have put it—cannot be overestimated. The next morning, when Constantine told me we were going ahead with the suit, he was as happy as a clam at high tide.

The take-home here is that for outside presidents, MIT is a tough row to hoe. It isn't enough to love your job. You have to make the faculty love that it is you who is doing it.

6 Housemaster

I became housemaster of Senior House in 1981. Constantine Simonides was the one who offered me the job. Constantine later became a very close friend and advisor. You might not have predicted that if you had been a fly on the wall when he offered me the job. To put it bluntly, when I became housemaster at Senior House, the dormitory was functioning as a storm drain for the other MIT living groups. All the difficult students were funneled there. These were the students who were incapable of living harmoniously in the more normal dorms. These were the students who snatched fire extinguishers off the walls and ran down the corridors spraying their housemates' doors.

Or else they were the students who were attracted to the special character of the place from the get-go. During orientation week students filtered through all the dormitories seeking the living group that fit them best. This was a peculiarity of MIT, this business of Residence/Orientation (R/O) week. At the time, most colleges and universities assigned freshmen to a single dorm devoted to the freshman year. That was it! No choice. After living there for a year they would choose other living arrangements. Not so at MIT. A week before classes began, students came on campus and chose where they would like to live for the next four years by visiting the dormitories, fraternities, sororities, and independent living groups. R/O week was a chaos of living arrangement management during which fraternities, sororities, and independent living groups on and off campus vied for the affections of the incoming class so their beds would be filled and their expenses for the year met. Think a thousand freshmen roaming around going to parties, dances, smokers, nonsmokers, what have you. MIT participated in this rite of residence because it didn't have enough beds to house the incoming freshman class. It relied on the 350 or so nondormitory beds to help accommodate each class. This led, in my view, to an intolerable situation, but let me save that for another chapter.

The culture of Senior House was special, and it attracted certain students like flies to, well, honey. The ones who didn't like honey were actually in tears if they were told that they were unable to have their first or second choice and that, alas, they had to be assigned to their last choice, Senior House. More often than not these students had their parents step in and threaten to withdraw their children from MIT if their room assignments weren't changed. They were invariably transferred out. I couldn't blame them for crying or going.

Constantine didn't tell me any of this in our talks before I took the job. I can understand why. His back was against the wall. The fall semester was about to start and no one was willing to take the job. Being the head of a graduate department, I was sufficiently outside the undergraduate system not to have picked up on the vibes. I certainly didn't do due diligence, as they say. To make matters worse, my best friend, Morris Halle, advised me to take the job. He saw it, pure and simple, as a way of increasing my salary. After all, the apartment in Senior House came with the job. It was a perk. Morris couldn't know, nor could I, that what looked like a sinecure would turn out to be an "unrest cure" (thanks to H. H. Munro a.k.a. Saki). To put it differently, as my mother used to say, "Constantine saw me coming."

I took the job. I forgave Constantine. I came to love him, but, even so, it was low rent not to have told me what to expect.

The position is a live-in arrangement, with the housemaster having an apartment located in the dormitory itself. My then wife, Margaret, and I had been residents for less than a week when we were visited by the house president. I remember what he looked like. He had the puffy look of an MIT antinerd, someone who worked very hard at his studies, didn't get enough sleep, ate too much pizza, and drank too much beer on the weekends. He had adopted the practiced mien of a hard-bitten leader of the working classes, namely, his fellow antinerd nerds in Senior House. He had thick, black hair and a swarthy complexion. When he came into my apartment, I felt as if I were being boarded by a pirate.

After a very few pleasantries—basically an exchange of names—he came straight to the point.

"Your job as housemaster," he said, "is to stay in this apartment and mind your own business. We'll let you know when we need your help."

"We?" I asked.

"The grease," he said. "The house grease."

This was the name for the Senior House government, all elected grease.

"What kind of help?" I asked.

"We may need you to run interference for us with them," and he jerked his head in a direction that I took to mean the rest of MIT. (This incident helped me begin to understand the role of hacking at MIT, but I'll save that for later as well.)

"I'll do my best to be fair," I said.

He gave me an odd look as if to say, "What the hell has that got to do with it?"

My first introduction to the residents, the nongrease, was equally unsettling. The other housemasters had advised us that the first order of business was opening up lines of communication with the students. Food, I was told, was always a good way to go. So the second Saturday after moving in, Margaret and I arranged to have a picnic in the courtyard. It was a "Meet Your Housemasters" kind of event.

We arranged to barbecue hot dogs and hamburgers outdoors. There were soft drinks and ice cream. I was standing behind the grill when two Senior House sophomores came up for hot dogs. While I was preparing them, I made what I hoped would be ice-breaking remarks.

What follows is virtually a transcript of that early conversation. The course the students were talking about was a legendary introductory course in computer science taught by one of MIT's best undergraduate teachers, Gerald Sussman. The course was first taught in 1980. Jerry taught it for seventeen years before going on to newer things. In its day it was an MIT highlight, the basis for a book that shared its title with the course itself, *Structure and Interpretation of Computer Programs*. I often saw Jerry marching toward the classroom wearing a white Stetson hat and followed by a small parade of teaching assistants. The group looked like an academic version of *Make Way for Ducklings* with the chief duck dressed like a cowboy.

MIT students typically refer to their courses, like their classrooms, by numbers rather than names. So I asked, "What do you think of 6.001?"

1st student: "It's a great course. The best so far."

2nd student: "I think it sucks."

1st student: "Fuck you."

2nd student: "Fuck you."

They turned away from me and went their separate ways. I stood there with two hot dogs in my hand and my mouth open. I had heard that MIT undergraduates were undersocialized, but it never occurred to me that they could be so succinct about it.

Paul Gray always thought that one of the most important things he ever did as president was to increase the number of undergraduate women at the Institute. That was, indeed, a major and long-overdue change. It had a number of salutary effects, not least of which was socializing an undersocialized male menagerie. One reliable indicator was vandalism in the living groups. Repair costs fell dramatically once significant numbers of women moved in.

During my first year someone had—Lord knows why—torn the banister of one of the living area staircases out of the wall. Of course no one confessed. The graduate student residents, known as tutors, who lived with the undergrads as on-the-spot guidance counselors, were aping the three monkeys. Their view was that if they ratted on the students, the students would never trust them again. It was clear that many of them viewed themselves as working for the students even though the Institute was paying the bills.

I was furious. Maybe it was my Old Testament sense of right and wrong that was eating at me. After all, it wasn't my money at stake. But it really bugged me that someone was tearing banisters out of the wall and getting away with it. It especially bugged me because I saw these students as highly privileged children whose prospects in life were head and shoulders above those of the kids living in the projects just outside the Institute's precincts. When they should have been thanking their lucky stars they were saved from that, they were, instead, trashing the place.

When it happened a second time, I decided it was no more Mr. Nice Guy. I asked the house to rat on the perp. Again no one came forward. I announced that the cost of repair was a thousand dollars and that each and every resident of the house would be charged his or her portion for the repairs. It came to about $5.50 per student. Even at that low price, the assessment was totally unfair. But my sense of fairness had wilted in the heat. Later that same day, under cloak of guaranteed anonymity, someone came to my apartment and told me who the culprit was. He paid.

The good news was that the culprit was brought to account. The bad news was that I had broken the covenant the house president thought he had made with me. I was supposed to stay in my apartment until the grease needed me. Going after someone who ripped banisters out of walls was not part of the agreement. So I was no longer their housemaster. I was their house-adversary. I admit this must have been tough for them to take. That didn't bother me. The Senior House activists were not in my eyes a likable lot.

During our first week at Senior House, Margaret, my fifteen-year-old son, and I were invited to join the students to help decorate the second floor of Runkle, one of Senior House's six entries. Named after the second president of MIT, John Daniel Runkle, it is the tallest of the entries (six floors); all the others—Ware, Atkinson, Holman, Nichols, Crafts—are four stories high. Each of the entries had developed its own special subculture. On that particular evening, I had no idea what to expect as we crossed the courtyard, negotiating our way past the tire swing that hung from a huge tree in the courtyard like a talisman around the symbolic neck of the house.

We walked up the steps to the second floor of Runkle. In retrospect I think the denizens of the entry managed to get what they wanted out of the visit. I was scandalized. A perfectly clean and newly painted hallway was being turned into some kind of Goth antechamber. They were painting the neat and illuminated white walls black. When we arrived, they were in the midst of applying their own designs to the blackness as well as slogans like Mucho Tokes for Sport Death Folks. That's not a direct quote. I made it up. But you get the idea. There were psychedelic emblems all along the corridor and murals at one end, some of them quite well done. When I stepped into the hallway, a faint blue haze floated just below the ceiling like a low-hanging cloud. It seemed to seep out from behind closed doors.

One of the students stuck a paintbrush in my hand. Like the emergency signals on the radio, this was clearly a test. Expecting something far more traditional, like tea and cakes and would I like one lump or two, I found myself forced to participate in a Sherman-Williams satanic rite.

"Do you have any yellow paint?" I asked. They did.

I drew a big picture of Donald Duck on the wall. It was a cartoon figure I had maniacally copied over and over again while I was lying in bed with scarlet fever as a child. It seemed the appropriate image for the evening. Underneath the figure of Uncle Donald in great yellow letters I wrote "Runkle Duck." I saw myself as decorating the Senior House nursery.

This was my third introduction into the culture of Senior House. It was a kind of baptism by paintbrush. I learned later that the practice was part of an antirush atmosphere that the Runkle students concocted at the beginning of each school year. The idea was to attract Senior House types and scare away the squares. Presumably painting the corridor to resemble one of Dante's circles of hell was deemed an effective screen. Senior House had its own little admissions committee. That was why each fall, after Physical Plant employees painted the walls of the corridors outside the dorm rooms white, the denizens of Runkle repainted them black.

I believe the painting incident made us Public Enemy No. 1 in the eyes of several Runkle residents. The next year I sent a note to the paint party planners strongly discouraging antirush activities. That sparked a kangaroo court that made *Lord of the Flies* look like "The Three Little Pigs." I'll get to that.

A few weeks after the painting party we received reports that one of the students in the entry next to ours was hearing voices. I called the entry's tutor.

"Why haven't you told us or gotten him to Medical?" I asked.
"We take care of our own," he said.

This was an example of the "What happens in Vegas stays in Vegas" attitude that I had picked up from my visit with the house president a few weeks earlier. We managed to get the student into Medical but not before he went walking out in the middle of the night in his underwear saying that he was going to visit the dean for student affairs.

This business of "taking care of our own" was one more manifestation of the Senior House "them vs. us" culture. It was maddening to try to get the house members to do something as rational as seeking help for one another when help was needed and available. In fact, the infirmary was less than a football field away. But the kinds of contortions one had to go through to get a needy student there were extraordinary. Medical was seen as akin to a waste disposal plant straight out of *Soylent Green*. That attitude, by the way, wasn't unique to Senior House.

On one occasion a member of the house had a serious reaction to LSD, a bad trip. When we found out about it, we went to the student's room. We were told that the students themselves were bringing the bad tripper back down. We wanted to take him over to Medical straightaway. But it wasn't that simple. Students had to seek medical help of their own volition. In this case the student's volition was hidden away inside some monstrous drug stupor. The student's friends said they would handle everything. This meant having someone sit with him in his room every hour of the day for the next several days until his faculties were restored. Rather than argue, we negotiated. It was the height of absurdity that we had to negotiate for the care of a student, but that's the way it was. The only alternative was to drag him out of the room. And neither he nor I was in any condition for that.

His caregivers agreed to take phoned-in advice from an expert, someone who could tell them what to expect at each stage of the recovery. So we called Medical ourselves, contacted the psychiatrist whose specialty was drug cases, and arranged for him to call in on a regular basis and talk with the student caregivers about how things were going.

The problem was that the recovery was taking longer than expected. After two days the caregivers began to lose interest. The press of classes and reading and exams took over. Soon enough, the myth of "We take care of our own" was trumped by "We take care of ourselves." The student recovered. My best recollection is that in the end he went to Medical. While my memory of the endgame is hazy, my sense of the infidelity of his caregivers remains intact.

To be fair, the infirmary wasn't always cooperative. Being a housemaster, I sometimes felt as if I were caught between the devil (Senior House) and the deep blue sea (Medical). One night a student called and asked me to come over to his room. Not surprisingly, it was on the second floor of Runkle. His girlfriend du jour seemed to be passing out periodically. He, at least, wanted help. When I reached the room, she seemed to be fine. Then, a few minutes after I arrived, sure enough, she fainted dead away. We caught her before she hit the floor, not an easy thing to do. She was on the heavy side and her boyfriend was thin as a rail. I picked up the phone and called Medical. The night nurse answered. It was around 10 p.m.

I identified myself and then said, "Can you send an ambulance to Senior House right away? A student has fainted in one of the dormitory rooms."

While I was on the telephone, the student suddenly sat up.

"Hold on," I said. "She's come around."

"If she's conscious," the nurse said, "we can't send an ambulance. Perhaps you can walk her over."

I told her I would try. I put down the phone.

"Shall we go over to Medical?" I asked.

No sooner were the words out of my mouth than the student passed out again. I picked up the phone and dialed Medical. The same night nurse answered.

"She's passed out again," I said. "Can you send that ambulance?"

Just then she came to again.

"Her eyes just opened," I said. "She seems to be passing in and out of consciousness."

"Well," said the night nurse, "if she's awake, we can't send an ambulance. You'll just have to bring her in yourself."

I hung up. I turned to the young woman and asked her if she felt well enough to walk to Medical. She said she didn't want to go.

"Why not?" I asked.

"I don't want to walk through all that marijuana smoke in the corridor."

"I'll try to clear the hallway," I said. "Maybe I can keep the door open or something."

Once again the words were hardly out of my mouth when she slumped to the floor.

I was at the phone in an instant. If I could get that ambulance here, I wouldn't have to worry about marijuana smoke.

"Quick," I said to the night nurse. "She's out like a light."

Just then, she came to again.

"Never mind," I said to the night nurse. I hung up and took the student by the arm.

"Take a deep breath and hold it," I said, and we rushed down the stairway and out into the courtyard. Luckily she stayed conscious long enough for me to walk her the half-block to the infirmary. She spent the night and returned to Senior House the next day.

Senior House was home to 183 undergrads and 5 graduate tutors. Over the years my beef was with about 40 of those students and a handful of the tutors. The other 140 students went about their business and rarely wondered what the fuss was about. But 40 hard-assed students were enough to make my life a misery. You might wonder why I stuck it out so long, why I remained housemaster for seven years? Well, the truth is, I wasn't going to let the bad guys win.

They had a pretty good run at it. Taking their cue straight out of *Lord of the Flies*, a small coterie of students mounted a campaign to oust Margaret and me from Senior House. They had been alienated by our position on pornography, our position on vandalism, our antidrug attitude, our anti-antirush stance, and, probably, Runkle Duck. (I hope so.) They held a number of anti-Keysers meetings, some of which we attended. Those culminated in one secret meeting at which they listed all their grievances against us. I call it "secret" because we wanted to be present to answer their charges. They refused. They taped the meeting and made a copy of the tape available at the reception desk along with a questionnaire designed to find out how many of the house residents wanted us out. The idea was to listen to the unanswered charges, then vote your conscience. To the best of my knowledge this organized campaign against housemasters on the part of a subset of the house residents was unprecedented in the history of MIT.

To my mind the meeting at which we were charged but were refused the opportunity to answer charges was the most astonishing thing that happened in seven years of astonishing Senior House things. This ditty, apologies to *The Music Man*, went through my mind:

Oh, we got mishigas
Right here in Senior City.
With a capital "M"
And that rhymes with "them."
And that stands for McCarthy.

It was as if the students had come up with the idea of a kangaroo court all by themselves. It was impressive as well as frightening. I marveled that this clutch of libertarians in the so-called bastion of "live and let live" could be so un-self-aware. That, I think, was at the heart of everything. The poet Robert Burns once wrote, "O would some power the giftie gie us to see ourselves as others see us." Amen!

There was another, more formal and open meeting. It was called, at the disaffected students' request, to discuss their charges. This open meeting, which took place on March 7, 1985, was summarized in an article in Vol. 1, No. 1 of the *Runkle Roar* dated March 15, 1985. I suspect the newspaper was created precisely because of the fuss that Margaret and I created around issues like pornography and drug use at Senior House.

The first issue contained—in column 1 no less—an article praising Margaret for attending to the "showerhead crisis." Physical Plant had decided to replace the old showerheads with more energy-efficient ones. It hadn't occurred to them that anyone would care. For goodness' sake, it was just a showerhead. The plan was put into place without asking, rather like routine maintenance. At Senior House we soon learned that nothing was "routine." Any non-Senior-House-initiated change was an unwelcome intrusion. Not surprisingly, then, the move to replace the old showerheads engendered a small uprising. Here is how a supportive writer described the situation in the *Runkle Roar*:

What happens when someone tries to save the students money by making the showers more efficient? The rats are so angry they try to bite the very hand that feeds them . . . their own housemasters.

I don't quite understand what happened. First, I thought people were joking. . . . I heard things like, "let's leave the water on," "it's all a plot," "let's have a shower party," and so on. I am guilty too, I suppose. I joined in the fun and I'm sure we all had a good laugh. But then I realized some people were taking the whole thing seriously. Too seriously. Consider these flames [that's Senior House speak for serious criticism]: "sit in the Keyser's shower," "pelt them with eggs and fruit" (or something like that) on the Runkle 4th flame sheet.

Come on, kids, grow up! Don't you even know they're on your side? Think! Who put up the petition asking for signatures of those wishing to keep the old showerheads? Who personal (sic) spoke to the only people who could help us? Who found out that "No one had any idea anybody wanted to keep the old showerheads." Who solved the problem less than three days after it came up?

Yes, we all know the answer. Margaret Keyser is probably the only person who could have done the job so swiftly. She correctly predicted the probable reaction of house residents and verified that feeling. She knew exactly whom to speak to, just before he left on vacation. She is well known and respected by other housemasters, housing office people, and other important people. It's a good thing she acted while the rats were still whimpering among themselves. It's too bad some people just don't appreciate how much she does for us.

In the very next issue of the *Runkle Roar* a correspondent replied, taking issue with the obvious support the writer had for Margaret:

And although I welcome the showerheads staying, to make Margaret Keyser into the patron saint of chrome for doing something that any house member with strong beliefs should feel compelled to do is, in my opinion, somewhat excessive.

That rebuttal was in column 1 of page 1. Columns 2 and 3 were taken up with a summary of the March 7 meeting. In attendance were the dean for student affairs, the associate dean for student affairs, the Senior House tutors, and eight to ten students. The meeting was requested by two students, both young women, who were up in arms about what they saw as a serious breach of contract between housemasters and residents of Senior House. One of their central accusations was that Margaret and I were narcs.

Senior House was definitely not a drug-free zone. By one informal survey, 83 percent of the students used marijuana at least once a week. A much smaller number, something like 3 percent, experimented with heavier drugs like laboratory-manufactured LSD. And at least once a year students managed to buy a keg of nitrous oxide and bring it into the house for partying. Less than 1 percent were into heavy drugs like cocaine. I never heard of a single heroin user. I doubt there was one.

Margaret, much to her credit, frequently walked through the corridors of the dormitory to discourage the public use of drugs. What students did in their own rooms was their own affair. But what they did outside was ours. This gave rise to the suspicion that we were narcs waiting to pounce. Even though neither of us ever brought charges against students for possession of drugs, their own paranoia was sufficient to demonize us.

I am not sure how organized the drug culture was in Senior House during the 1980s. But I had ominous glimpses. I remember one occasion when we invited a number of students to our apartment for soft drinks and cheese one Sunday afternoon. About thirty students were gathered. There was a knock at the door. When I opened it, I saw a man about thirty years old with a three-day stubble. He wore a black leather jacket, faded jeans, and sneakers with holes at the little toes. In short, he looked like the kind of guy I wouldn't want to meet in a hospital emergency room, let alone a dark alley. He asked for one of the students by name. The student had seen him at the door. The two of them left without a word. When they were gone, I looked out the window and saw a beat-up car parked in the president's house driveway next door. Two men were talking to the student. From my perch at my apartment window one floor above, I could see that they were not exchanging pleasantries. The men got into their car and backed out onto Memorial Drive, leaving the student standing there watching. Then the student walked away. He didn't come back to the party.

"I'll never see him again," I thought. I was being cynical. Maybe the whole thing was innocent. But it left me with an uneasy feeling as, in fact, did several incidents at Senior House.

During one of the infamous Steer Roasts that Senior House concocted as an annual bacchanalia to épater les bourgeois, I remember stepping outside the courtyard onto Memorial Drive. It was a Friday night. The music was agonizingly loud, de rigueur for young people then as well as now. The president's house was next door and in front of the house was a tree. Standing behind the tree—lurking was more like it—was the figure of a man deep in the shadows.

"Are you all right?" I said.

The figure just stood there. He didn't say a word.

"Do you need any help?"

More silence. It could, of course, have been anybody, a panhandler, a homeless person, even a plainclothes detective. Suddenly it came over me that it wasn't too smart to be querying someone hiding in the shadows and not answering back when I spoke. If he was a supplier, I thought, I'd better go back inside where, despite the bacchanalia of the courtyard, it suddenly seemed the safer place to be. These were merely intimations, of course. They wouldn't stand up in a court of law. Others would.

One involved a student who publicly acknowledged that he had had a bad trip using LSD. He sought medical help at MIT. He had been experiencing unpleasant flashbacks for several months. These came at unexpected moments and with enough frequency to make it impossible for him to continue his studies. Both he and his doctor decided that the best thing was for him to fly home to the West Coast until the flashbacks wore off. I'm told that in some cases that never happens. In any case this particular student didn't come back while I was at Senior House.

It was MIT's practice not to allow students who were on medical leave, as it were, to fly home alone. The Institute bought a pair of tickets, one way for him and round trip for Margaret, who was to accompany him. Before he left, he told us he would like to speak to a group of students who lived in his entry, his closest neighbors. He wanted us to host the meeting in our apartment. He wanted, he said, to warn them against taking LSD. He wanted to tell them what was happening to him. We agreed.

On the appointed day about a dozen of his friends and entry-mates assembled in our apartment along with him, his doctor, Margaret, and me. He began by telling everyone that he was unable to continue taking classes and why. He started to talk about the flashbacks, what they were doing to him, how he couldn't control them when they came. As he spoke, he became more and more agitated. Suddenly, he stopped speaking altogether. He looked helplessly at his doctor. Sizing up the situation, the doctor put an arm around his shoulders and walked him back to Medical.

As he left, the doctor said, "It's a flashback."

Surely, I thought, seeing a student in the actual throes of a painful drug experience would be some sort of deterrent. I asked the remaining students if their friend's experience would have any effect on them. They all said no. Even though the likelihood of their telling me how they really felt was about the same as their offering to clean their dorm rooms, I had a strong sense that they greeted their friend's disclosure with the feeling that he just couldn't handle it, but they could.

I suppose the hardest evidence that drug usage at Senior House was alive and well was the March 7, 1985, meeting with the two deans, the tutors, and the complainants. The two student leaders of the complainants argued that Senior House residents didn't trust their housemasters. The reason was that the housemasters encouraged "narcing" by tutors. As the first issue of the *Runkle Roar* reported:

After failing to establish any specific point of wrongdoing the point was made that people feel that the Keysers will act against people who they know to use drugs and that this will drive people away from communications with the housemasters. As of yet, however, there has been no clear evidence of policing. [The Senior House president] characterized the situation accurately when he said 'The policing is in your head.'

The second issue of the *Runkle Roar* published an analysis of the questionnaire given out to house residents on March 17, 1985. The article noted that we had lost the "stay or leave" question 44 to 42, adding "the fact remains that, out of 181 house residents only 86 gave an opinion one way or the other to that question and it cannot be said that 44-42 margin represents a consensus in house opinion." The writer reasoned:

The conclusion to be reached from this information is that the results of the questionnaire are not a demand for the Keysers to leave, but for a modification in policy, especially in the area of their dealings with residents who use drugs. This lends credence to the position taken by a number of students who say that there is a problem in that there is a perception that the Keysers are hostile to drug users.

Duh. You're damned right we were hostile to drug users. The use of drugs is a criminal offense. As an agent of MIT, I was obliged to uphold the law. The students at Senior House honestly believed that it was reasonable for them to ask me to aid and abet criminal activity. That is what was interesting about this whole brouhaha. It was not that the Keysers were bastards and the students who hated us wanted us out. It was their sense of entitlement. Senior House students had the right to break the law *and* they had the right to expect their housemasters to help them. They weren't looking for housemasters. They were looking for accomplices. What planet were they living on?

As it happens, I was in favor of legalizing drug usage. But I was not in favor of breaking the law. As an agent of MIT, I saw that I had no choice but to push drug usage back behind the doors of the dorm rooms. There the students could do what they damned well pleased. But as soon as drugs were in the stairways, the corridors, the courtyards, it became a public issue. That was the heart of the matter. The students saw no boundary between the privacy of their rooms and the public character of the corridors and courtyard. They really believed they were at home.

I stepped down as housemaster in 1988, ten years before I retired from the Institute. Five years later, in 1993, Margaret and I were officially divorced. In all, twenty-two years have gone by since I left Senior House. I have not been able to bring myself to go back for a visit nor, I hasten to add, have I ever been invited. The lore of the house, I learned in the course of writing this book, is that Senior House was responsible for the breakup of my marriage. That wasn't true. But I can see why that myth might have been empowering to the students who first believed it back in the 1980s. No, the reason why I haven't returned to the house is the same reason why many soldiers don't return to their last battlefield. There are just too many ghosts.

It's just as well. The most recent housemasters—they have since left MIT for the other coast—appear on the Web in Steer Roast photographs, mud-wrestling in the courtyard while the house looks on approvingly. Perhaps that's what it takes to be a successful housemaster at Senior House. You have to get down and dirty with the students—literally.

7 Pornography and Free Speech

Paul Gray became president of MIT in 1980. Undergraduate women made up something like 16.5 percent of the student body. Five years later, thanks to Paul, a third of the incoming class was women. Today the number is close to half. This shift in the character of the undergraduate population had a profound effect on MIT though, at the time, no one really realized what was happening. It was as if MIT were a ship on the ocean while a tidal wave was passing underneath. One tiny indicator was the change in my job title. I began my tenure with the title associate provost for educational policy and programs. That was in 1985. Four years later it changed to associate provost for Institute life. The title change reflected the change in the nature of my job. In the beginning I was supposed to worry about undergraduate education, but the culture shift that was gripping MIT caused me to become more and more invested in issues like sexual harassment, pornography, and free speech and less and less with educational matters.

In retrospect the focus on pornography and harassment was not surprising. As the number of undergraduate women at the Institute grew, showing pornographic films on Registration Day, a time-honored undergraduate tradition, was no longer taken for granted. Graduate women, now sensitive to the power of women united, began to oppose sexual harassment in their part of MIT. Soon the movement reached into the postdoctoral world. Instead of focusing on undergraduate education, I found myself MIT's man in court. I have to admit that it was interesting, but it sure as hell wasn't what I had signed on for. The message of Tolstoy's vast novel *War and Peace* can be put into one iambic trimeter: you can't control events. I take this to be a candidate for my epitaph along with: Beneath this stone lies S. J. Keyser, who knows what's beyond and is none the wiser.

I'm not complaining, by the way. I found being in court incredibly interesting and something that would never have happened to me had I not been a senior administrator. One case I remember especially involved a world-famous faculty member and a postdoctoral associate. The latter had accused the former of all manner of bad behavior, including stealing her ideas. At the heart (pun intended) of the matter was an alleged extramarital affair. It fell to me to try to mediate the conflict. I failed. She took him to court. I was on hand as MIT's representative along with Jerry Weinstein, an MIT lawyer, who worked with the firm of Palmer and Dodge, the external law firm that for all intents and purposes functioned as MIT's in-house counsel.

Jerry is a tall, thin, handsome man with a boyish mop of curly hair that makes him look as if he had just stepped out of the shower—that and twenty years younger. He is soft-spoken and, unlike so many lawyers I have encountered over the years, he is anything but in your face. Talking to him is like talking to a hypnotist who is always smiling. He is laid back and to this day I can't recall him having a bad word to say about any of les misérables we had to deal with. Jerry is always dressed well—dark blue pinstriped suits, dazzling white shirts, and a tie as unobjectionable as his manner. In short, he is one of the best lawyers I have ever had the pleasure of doing business with.

Jerry and I had become quite good friends due to our frequent pairing on matters that involved complainants, respondents, and the Institute. My wife, Nancy, and I socialized with him and his wife. They were ardent *Sopranos* fans. Nancy and I didn't own a television set. That was enough to launch a dinner invitation and an evening of *Sopranos* watching. I have to say the TV show didn't hold a candle to the day Jerry and I spent in court.

One of the major parties in the matter is now dead. So, too, is the judge. Thinking about that makes me feel old since I was older than all of them. On the day of the trial Jerry and I met at MIT and rode over to the Middlesex County Superior Courthouse together. I have always been impressed by the contrast between the entrance to the courthouse and the courtrooms. The entrance is a bit trashy. The entrance hall looks the worse for wear. Rough-looking people are scattered around leaning against walls and looking either furtive, or uncomfortable, or both. They seem to be in conversation either with their lawyers, family members, or themselves. The guard at the entrance checks everyone for weapons. I remember having to leave my tiny Swiss Army knife with him.

By contrast the courtrooms on the sixth floor are all board-room airs and quiet decorum with lots of imposing mahogany woodwork and barren maple benches. This morning only a few of us were present: the complainant and her lawyer, the defendant and his lawyer, Jerry, and me. We all rose when the judge entered the room. She took me by surprise. I had expected to see a tall, aristocratic figure projecting an above-it-all hauteur. Instead, I saw a short woman built like a fireplug in a black robe. She mounted the steps, disappeared momentarily from view, only to pop up again behind the bench.

The opening remarks were concluded. Then, suddenly and apparently a surprise to everyone, the judge called a recess and asked Jerry and me to step into her chambers. When we entered, she was sitting in a large, black, stuffed leather chair that made her seem even smaller. I stood in front of her, ill at ease but at the same time mesmerized by the dignity of it all. This was the real thing. This was the majesty of the law come to a fireplug of a judge in a black leather chair. Here was where the buck stopped. I fidgeted a bit, shifting my weight from one foot to the other. She must have noticed. She offered a few pleasantries. Then she paused, eyed me and then Jerry and said, "She loves him. She wants him dead."

That, after an entire year of to-ing and fro-ing, of anguished phone conversations, of long awkward silences with both parties, was the whole ugly mess summed up in seven Anglo-Saxon monosyllables.

That, I think, was the moment when I developed my great respect for the Massachusetts system of judicial selection. The judge was right. There was absolutely no sense in going through with a trial.

We went home, talked settlement, and put the matter to rest, not without MIT paying and not without the defendant paying as well. Whatever the price, it was worth it.

She loves him. She wants him dead.

A few years later the defendant died.

The clash of male versus female cultures at MIT, which had reached all the way to the Middlesex County Superior Courthouse, was alive and well on campus. It was certainly evident during my first year at Senior House. The dormitory did its level best to maintain its position as an outlier among MIT dorms. It was the place where all the cool stuff happened, everything from sex, drugs, and rock and roll to Steer Roast. (I'll come to that in a moment.) The students captured their credo in a banner that consisted of a ragged bedsheet with a death's head painted on it. The death's head floats on a black background and is decorated with the stars and stripes of the American flag. The teeth of the death's head spell out the slogan Only Life Can Kill You. The words "Sport Death" painted in big, white letters curl around the skull's jawbone like a scraggly bowtie.

The meaning of "Sport Death" defined on the Web site of one of the house's former citizens was reproduced in the Internet's Urban Dictionary, warts and all. I copy it in full here:

MIT - "Sport Death" meant roughly: "do not settle for mediocracy; live life in extremeus (sic),"or something like that. The practical expression of this philosophy involved intoxication, wild parties, ear-splitting rock-n-roll, and polymorphous sexual activity.

Like bumper stickers at a political convention, Sport Death was all over Senior House during freshman orientation week, the time when students chose the living groups they would like to be in. The Sport Death banner flew from the fifth floor of Runkle. Students wore T-shirts with the logo displayed on their chests. Outside on Ames Street, the house facade contained two empty niches that at one time must have held decorative statues. On at least one occasion that I can remember Senior House denizens placed themselves in these niches and stood like Greek statues for as long as they could manage it, draped in Sport Death togas. This was how the house advertised itself to the incoming freshmen. The Senior House students left no doubt about the kind of comrades they wanted.

Naturally I was curious about the Sport Death motto. I asked one of the house officers where it came from. He told me that some years earlier several residents of the house went skydiving. One student's parachute didn't open. He had leaped to his death. The next day his friends went right back up into the air and continued skydiving, thumbing their noses at death, as it were, daring the demon to off them. He told the story with passion. I was impressed, but not so impressed that I didn't inquire of the dean's office the name of the Senior House student who hurtled to his death while skydiving.

I wasn't surprised to learn that no student had ever per-
ished in such a fashion, either from Senior House or any other
house at MIT. In other words, Sport Death, the Senior House
credo, was an urban myth. I brought that to the attention of the
house every chance I got. (I am surprised only forty-four voted
for ousting me.) It made no difference. These students—among
America's best young scientific minds—were perfectly capable of
mentally filing away under the rubric of true things the second
law of thermodynamics and the myth of Sport Death.

Over the years there were a number of battles with students,
all of which were wrapped in the Sport Death mantle. The issues
were really two, sex and drugs. Rock and roll was there as well,
but it tagged along like the tail on a Tasmanian devil. Every
spring, as a rite of passage, the students staged an event called
"Steer Roast." It was a low-rent bacchanalia. They set up a barbecue pit in the courtyard, bought a cow, skewered it on a rotating
spit, and spent a day and a night roasting it. A number of rooms
in the house were set aside for illicit activities—bondage, drugs,
and, of course, pornography.

Pornography was a constant raw spot at Steer Roast. In the
same issue of the *Runkle Roar* (March 15, 1985, Vol. 1, No. 1) that
I quoted from earlier, the following editorial appeared:

You may have noticed a little box at the desk asking for your opinion
on pornography at Steer Roast. Once again the house is going through
the motions of what has become a rite of spring over the past few years.
Trees and flowers come into bloom, students make plans to go to Flori-
da, the baseball season begins and Senior House has a vote on pornography. Every year there is great flaming over this issue and every year those
dirty movies get an overwhelming vote of confidence from the house. It
is extremely unlikely that this year will be any different.

We believe this issue has been dead for a long time. The Keysers are
fighting a hopelessly losing battle which services no goal except to increase the ranks of those who seek to replace them. They should admit
defeat. It would save all of us a lot of time and effort.

Those "dirty movies" weren't the only manifestation of Senior House's "overwhelming" predilection for two-dimensional sex. One of the major events of the Steer Roast afternoon was the ceremonial designation of the year's Virgin Killer. The award included copies of hard-core porn magazines, hard-core because the magazine was sure to have a sexually explicit cover photograph.

The first year I had the pleasure of attending Steer Roast, the award and the magazine were given to the Senior House male who had slept with the greatest number of Senior House women in the preceding year. It was not unusual for the award to be given by a female house officer. As it happened, our house manager was a woman. She had a fourteen-year-old daughter. The house officers invited them both to the afternoon picnic. I asked those running the event not to give the Virgin Killer award when the young girl was present. They refused. I asked them to inform the house manager of what they intended to do. They failed to do that as well. When the time came, the award was bestowed and the cover of the magazine displayed in a slow arc to the house residents standing around like admirers at a rock concert, the house manager's daughter included.

I knew that this kind of insensitivity was characteristic of young people. I was also aware that many if not all of these young people would probably grow into relatively decent human beings in ten years. Still, I was appalled at their blindness to the wreckage they were leaving on the path to their maturity. There seemed to be no end to it.

A major Steer Roast event was the showing of a full-length pornographic film. I hadn't realized that was part of the ritual until early in the spring of my first year as housemaster, about a month before the actual event. Oddly enough, in a house that promoted an egalitarian line, there was no forum where I could engage the students in a debate about the practice. I asked the house officers how I might best express my opinion about show-ing a pornographic film at Steer Roast.

"Post a broadsheet on each of the entry doors," was the answer from one of the house officers. So I did.

Here is what I wrote:

23 April 1982

Dear Senior House Residents:

I have learned that part of the up-coming Steer Roast Activities includes the showing of pornographic films. I am writing to protest this activity and to explain the reasons for my protest.

I believe that these films are exploitative of and abusive to women. Because they are devoid of human feeling, these films reduce women to the status of inanimate objects. They are abusive because of the way women are mistreated in the manufacturing of these films.

If you feel that these films are exploitative of women, but if you are in favor of these films beings shown at Senior House, then you are indirectly supporting the abuse and exploitation of women in particular and of sexism in general. In this regard your support is quite tangible since these films must be procured with Senior House funds.

I would like to urge all of you to consider seriously what it means for Senior House to have such a tradition and then to consider abolishing it.

My immediate suggestion is that you contact those charged with implementing this sexist tradition and object strongly to its implementation this year. Toward this end I have prepared a petition to be presented to the house officers and to the relevant committee. This petition is available for your signature in my apartment.

Samuel Jay Keyser

I expected a reasoned broadsheet to appear on my apartment door. Instead, the response was limited to comments scrawled across my posting. Here is a selection of them:

1. Go away, Jay!

2. Your points are obviously true, but if people here want to be low, don't interfere!

3. Keyser is a candidate for most obnoxious freshman, no?

4. Be serious, Jay. This year we debated having cartoons instead of porn. Due to majority opposition, we elected to retain the sleeze (*sic*). If more people were convinced, the tradition can be changed. If not, we maintain our commitment to obscenity, sleeze, porn.

5. So maybe Jay is not so dumb.

Thank goodness for No. 5. Whoever wrote it (I never found out) added the explanatory note, in case anyone might have missed it, "one resident's support."

One morning shortly after the broadsheet appeared, one of the house officers stopped me in the courtyard. It was the same one who had suggested I post a broadsheet Martin Luther–like on the entry doors. I was on my way to my office.

"What right do you have to judge us?" he demanded.

"I have every right to judge you," I replied. "Just as you have a right to judge me."

"No, you don't," he argued. "You are like a policeman in this house. You have relinquished any right to judge."

His comment astonished me, a house officer likening the role of a housemaster to that of a policeman, this from a Sport Death-ster. What I should have said was, "In that case you're under arrest for stupidity." Instead I decided to take a different tack.

"You and I can agree on one thing," I said. "I am a son of a bitch. OK? Now let's talk about the content of my argument. By paying good money for a pornographic film, you and your fel-low officers are supporting an industry that dehumanizes people in general and women in particular. Do you really want to be doing that?"

He was apoplectic. "This is a democratic house," he said.

"If that's so," I replied, "why aren't there any gay porno flicks on the program?"

The way I saw it, Senior House, far from being an exemplar of freedom and abandon, was a bastion of male domination in avant-garde clothing. The hypocrisy was stifling.

Needless to say, the students showed their pornographic film at Steer Roast.

One night a few years after the broadsheet incident I received a call from a Senior House resident, a young woman.

"Did you know that LSC is going to show a porn film on Registration Day?" she asked.

The LSC, the Lecture Series Committee, was and is a student-run extracurricular activity that orchestrates special events for the MIT community: movies, speakers, and, as it turned out, on every Registration Day, a pornographic movie that was shown in a large central location on the MIT campus.

"No," I said. "I didn't."

"What are you going to do about it?"

"What are *you* going to do about it?" I wanted to ask right back.

I didn't. I had, by this time, formed an opinion about the emerging role of women at MIT. It was based on an incident I had heard about in another dormitory. Every year this dormitory held a Sex Goddess contest. Women in the dormitory were judged on their ability to perform sexually loaded tasks—for example, how quickly and well they licked whipped cream off the surface of phallus-shaped balloons. The winner was named Sex Goddess, a name that bestowed reward—she was a goddess—and contempt—she was not Athena, goddess of wisdom.

I was in therapy at the time and I often found myself posing questions to my shrink that were only tangentially related to my reasons for being there. In this case I asked him, in retrospect rather naively, why women were willing to debase themselves so much.

"The need to belong is terribly powerful," he said. "If this is what the MIT culture requires of them, then that's what they will do."

It wasn't hard for me to understand this. That's why I didn't ask the Senior House woman, "What are *you* going to do about it?" I knew that with a phone call to me she was already pushing the envelope.

The next day I got hold of the student head of the LSC.

"Is it true you're going to show a pornographic film on Reg Day?" I asked.

"Sure," he replied.

"Why?" I asked.

Over the phone I was putting on my game face. I braced myself for a lecture on "free speech" and what the hell business was it of mine anyway. I was in for a surprise.

"It's a money maker," the chairman said. "We make enough money off the Reg Day movie to fund most of our activities for the rest of the year."

"Really?" I was taken aback. "How much do you bring in?"

"About $2,500," he said.

I had to admit his capitalistic instincts were refreshing, coming as I did from what I felt was a hotbed of hypocrisy.

"I'll give you $3,000 not to show it," I said.

There was a moment of silence on the line and then the voice on the other end said, "It's a deal."

On Registration Day in September 1985, the LSC, breaking with tradition, showed *The Adventures of Buckaroo Banzai—Across the Eighth Dimension*. The student newspaper, the *Tech*, thought it important enough to report on the matter, adding, perhaps nostalgically, "LSC last showed an X-rated film, *The Opening of Misty Beethoven*, in March."

As associate provost, I had $13,000 of so-called walking-around money, discretionary funds I could use any way I saw fit. Three thousand dollars of it bought me a whole semester's worth of time to worry about the larger issue of pornography at the Institute. It also taught me that the profit motive was alive and well among the undergraduates.

Nineteen eight-seven was the year when I was literally thrown into the pornographic ring. The groundwork for the battle had been laid in 1984, when MIT implemented a policy requiring films of questionable pedigree to be vetted by a screening committee populated by students, faculty, and staff. According to the policy approved by MIT's highest authority, the Academic Council, without that screening committee's imprimatur a questionable (read "possibly pornographic") film could not be shown at MIT. In a town that housed both Alan Dershowitz and Harvey Silverglate, this was like pitching underhanded to Ted Williams. Dershowitz's nephew, Adam, decided to challenge the policy. I was caught up in the challenge.

Reminiscing over lunch twenty years later, John Deutch, my boss at the time, said, "I set you up, didn't I?"

His tone had a fair amount of compassion in it, though I couldn't say the same for the smile on his face.

"It was a dirty job," I replied. "Somebody had to do it."

It was, indeed, a dirty job. For one thing I thought MIT's policy was a bad one. It has always been my experience that the best way to effect cultural change at the Institute is simply to talk about it. The worst thing is to try to change the culture by enforcing rules.

That is what MIT's pornography policy did. The policy stated, among other things, that "any group or individual planning to show a sexually explicit film must notify the Office of the Dean for Student Affairs (ODSA) of this intent at least six weeks prior to the proposed showing date." Talk about red flags to freedom-of-speech bulls.

In my view not only was the policy completely against the grain of what I saw as a "let's-talk-about-it" culture, but it was also counterproductive. It shifted the conversation away from what pornography was about to a conversation about freedom of speech. It was only a matter of time before someone challenged the policy.

The inevitable challenge came on February 2, 1987, when Adam Dershowitz, the nephew of Alan Dershowitz, the well-known Harvard law professor, showed *Deep Throat* at an MIT dormitory. Adam was an undergraduate at the time, class of 1989. He chose the film and the venue—East Campus was the name of the dormitory—shrewdly. The City of Cambridge had already judged the film not to be obscene by its own community standards. Would MIT, then, take umbrage at the showing of a film in one of the public rooms of one of its own dormitories, a film that could be shown anywhere in Cambridge?

The answer was yes. Adam showed the film. James Tewhey, the associate dean for student affairs, subsequently brought charges. The relevant MIT committee, the Committee on Discipline (COD), heard the case. Paul Joss, a professor of physics, was chair of the committee. Alan Dershowitz accompanied his nephew to the proceedings. He was not permitted to appear as counsel for his nephew as a matter of Institute policy. However, he was admitted to the proceedings as an expert witness on "freedom of speech." Needless to say, it was no surprise that the committee found Adam Dershowitz innocent. The COD ruling said that the Institute's policy with respect to sexually explicit films "constitutes an excessive restraint on freedom of expression and . . . is therefore inappropriate for MIT." The COD declared the policy null and void and Adam free of any violation.

This threw the MIT administration into a tailspin. The COD had made a new policy by declaring, in effect, that students did not have to submit films to the screening committee "at least six weeks prior to the proposed showing date." The problem was that only the Academic Council had the right to set policy, not the COD. The Academic Council consists of all the very senior administrators at the Institute and is typically chaired by the president or, in the president's absence, the provost. The Dershowitz case had thrown a monkey wrench into MIT's governance machinery. It had never occurred to anyone to ask, "What do we do if a faculty committee flies in the face of a policy that has the Academic Council's imprimatur on it?" That loophole in MIT governance still exists, by the way. Every Institute committee has the potential for causing the governing machinery to grind to a halt simply by making policy instead of recommendations.

The matter was subjected to intense discussion among senior administrators. Bernard Frieden, then chair of the faculty, took the lead in drafting a new policy. In the end what MIT did was what any sane administration would do. It changed the policy. It pulled the prior restraint condition out of the porn policy the way Androcles pulled the thorn out of the lion's paw. It did something else. It wrote an amended policy which, like the Cheshire cat, would disappear in three years' time. That, as I recall, was John Deutch's idea. Today MIT has no pornography policy and, for the most part, no public pornography, except, of course, at Senior House where the need for two-dimensional sex continues to thrive.

I wish I could say it was as easy as that. Unfortunately, it wasn't. It took a long time between the COD pulling the plug on prior restraint and the writing and vetting of a new pornography policy. It was during that interim that John Deutch, to use his words, "set me up." Shirley McBay, the dean for student affairs, had been taking the brunt of the free speech attack on MIT's pornography policy for a couple of years. She had become the lightning rod. John thought she had done it long enough. He wanted someone else to take the heat.

The temperature was not long in rising. In a September 2, 1988, letter to the editor of the *Tech*, Adam Dershowitz announced his intention of showing *Deep Throat* in the Talbot Lounge of East Campus:

To the Editor:

On this coming Registration Day I will be showing *Deep Throat* in East Campus. My motivation for this showing is to eliminate the MIT Policy on Sexually Explicit Films.

I have chosen to show this film for several reasons, although it is offensive to some people. The controversy surrounding this film has made other people curious to see it to decide for themselves. In addition, there is a strong precedent at MIT and in Cambridge protecting the right to show this film.

I have challenged the policy before and won a strong victory before the Committee on Discipline. The policy is unenforceable and the COD ruled that it "constitutes an excessive restraint on freedom of expression at MIT and . . . the policy is therefore inappropriate for MIT."

Despite this ruling, the Academic Council acts as if the policy is still in effect and has chosen to ignore the decision of this group of students and faculty. The administration has chosen to let the contradictions over the policy stand, so we, the members of the MIT community, do not know what is acceptable. I will show this film to urge the administration's indecision over censorship to end.

The Constitution guarantees the right to freedom of speech. This right to freedom of expression, and choice of what to see, is protected even more strongly by Massachusetts law. An academic setting, such as MIT, should be open to all ideas and should set the highest standards for free expression.

I would like to invite and urge all members of the MIT community to exercise their constitutionally-granted right of choice on Registration Day. Decide for yourself whether to come to see this film (for entertainment, for political, educational, or other reasons), to protest this film, or not to come at all, but choose!

Do not leave it up to the Academic Council and the Pornography Screening Committee to decide what is appropriate for you to see, or not to see, when it is your right.

Adam L. Dershowitz

One week later I replied with a letter of my own:

To the Editor:

In the Sept. 2 issue of *The Tech*, Adam Dershowitz '89 announced his intention to show the film *Deep Throat* on the evening of Registration Day. Such a screening would be in violation of MIT's policy regarding the showing of sexually explicit films on campus.

Last year, the Committee on Discipline voiced disagreement with this policy. The Committee's action did not change or rescind the policy in question, however, and until such time as there are revisions to the policy, the current policy stands.

The issue here is not one of suppressing freedom of speech. MIT's policy does not prohibit the showing of any films on campus; rather it seeks to reflect MIT community standards with respect to when and where pornographic films are shown. When and where are important questions.

In this case, the point is to separate the showing of such films from the official occasions in the life of the community, such as Registration Day and especially Residence/Orientation week, when incoming students are being introduced to the culture and values of the MIT community. This matter does not have to do with academic freedom or free speech, but with decent conduct within a diverse, pluralistic university community.

Samuel J. Keyser
Associate Provost for Educational Programs and Policy

Three days later, on Monday evening, September 12, 1988, I went to East Campus to try to persuade Adam not to show the film. I was as successful in converting Adam as Isabella and Ferdinand were in converting the Jews.

When I entered East Campus, Adam was there. So were several women who lived in East Campus. I had a strong sense of being part of a ritual, as if I were an actor in a play written by somebody else. I think that was because there was no doubt in my mind how the evening would end.

I explained to Adam in a voice loud enough for everyone to hear that the dormitory was home to women as well as men, that knowing that they lived among men who watched pornography made them feel uneasy and unsafe. I asked him if we could talk about this in my office, if he could hold off showing the film until we had had a chance to discuss other options. Adam said that while he was sorry about the discomfort, there was a principle at stake. I told him that if he showed the film, I would be forced to write a letter of reprimand. He said he understood but that he had no choice. It was a matter of principle.

So there we were—two men, each doing what a man's gotta do. Adam showed the film. I sent the letter. Since the letter was between Adam and me and since, in any event, the Institute's policy was that upon graduation, such letters were expunged from the student's file, I won't quote the letter here except to say that I ended it by underlining that I thought this was a very serious matter. I am not sure why I added that last sentence except to underscore my conviction that the letter was, in fact, not a serious matter. I was protesting too much. The other options available to the Institute included suspension and expulsion. Placing a letter of reprimand in a student's folder that would, in effect, autodestruct in two years or whenever the student graduated, whichever came first, seemed mild in comparison.

I don't think Adam saw it that way. Certainly his lawyers didn't. Somewhere around the time of my letter—it may even have been before it was written—Adam made an appointment to see me. I remember the scene very well. The blackboard that hung on the wall next to the small round table that served as the site of the Project Interphase wrangle mentioned in the preface to this book was still there. We sat at the table, I facing the

blackboard and he to my left. I don't remember what we talked
about. But I do remember that he had a yellow legal pad. As the
conversation went on, I couldn't help but notice that he was
taking very careful notes. At one point I asked him why. He said
that since this matter could end up in court, he wanted to be
sure that he had recorded as accurately as possible what I had
to say.

At that point I was very clear about what I had to say. I said
the conversation was over.

Not long after that, his uncle, Alan Dershowitz, sent me a letter. I don't remember what it said. I do remember that it wasn't
very flattering and that it was written in a scrawling handwrit-
ing. I showed it to John Deutch. He said that if I answered it
he would break my arm. (John was always threatening to break
some part of my body.)

Dershowitz's letter to me was followed up by a letter that Harvey Silverglate, Adam Dershowitz's lawyer, had sent to the newly
minted president of MIT, Charles M. Vest. Silverglate also sent
a copy of that letter to members of the Corporation and, presumably to cover all the bases, to the student newspaper, which
reprinted it on Tuesday, February 5, 1990:

(Editor's note: *The Tech* received a copy of this letter addressed to President Charles M. Vest.)

I am writing to you in your capacity as a member of the MIT Corporation. I am at the same time writing to other Corporation members
as well. I am contacting you in my capacity as a cooperating attorney,
working through the Massachusetts Civil Liberties Union Foundation,
the local arm of the American Civil Liberties Union.

This letter is necessitated by the fact that I have been entirely unable
to deal fruitfully with the administration of MIT in a quest for what
MCLUF believes to be rather elemental justice due our client, Adam L.
Dershowitz G.

A member of the administration, Associate Provost Samuel J. Keyser,
has treated Dershowitz in an egregious manner, and MCLUF's efforts

to redress Dershowitz's grievance have been met with a refusal to take any remedial action. Instead, Keyser has insisted that I deal with his (or MIT's) legal counsel, Jerome N. Weinstein, of the Boston law firm of Palmer and Dodge.

In turn, Weinstein has told me that I might as well cease any efforts to redress the problem, since his client (it still remains unclear whether Weinstein is representing Keyser or MIT) refuses to do anything.

Since I am uncertain as to whether it is even ethically permissible for me at this point to deal with anyone within MIT's administration—in view of the fact that Weinstein is legal counsel and wishes me to deal with him rather than to deal directly with his client—I have taken the rather unusual step of contacting directly the body that is immediately above the Institute's administration, namely the Corporation.

Dershowitz, while an undergraduate at the Institute, sought to test an Institute-wide "policy" that restricted everyone's right—students and professors—to show sexually explicit films on campus, even to an audience of consenting people in a closed and hence private, non-intrusive setting.

When Dershowitz showed one "banned" film, *Deep Throat*, as a "test case," he was prosecuted within the Institute's disciplinary system. After an extensive hearing, the school's Committee on Discipline unanimously acquitted Dershowitz of the administration's charges, on the ground that the restrictive policy was a violation of academic freedom and that Dershowitz was acting within his rights.

Despite this acquittal, Keyser informed Dershowitz that the Institute's administration, or at least Keyser, considered the policy still to be in place and Dershowitz still to be bound by the policy. Dershowitz, again seeking a "test case," showed the same film the following year.

This time, instead of prosecuting him through the Institute disciplinary mechanism, Keyser simply made a decision, entirely on his own, that Dershowitz was in violation of a valid policy restricting his right to show the movie.

As a result, Keyser placed a letter of admonition in Dershowitz's student file for a period of time—an action that Keyser himself viewed as "serious."

Dershowitz, who is now a graduate student at the Institute, is simply trying to get acknowledgment placed in his file, to the effect that the admonition had been wrongly placed there. He did, after all, have a substantive right, secured by principles of academic freedom, to show the film.

Once re-prosecuted by Keyser for violation of a policy that a formal Institute disciplinary board had already declared to be in violation of academic freedom, Dershowitz had a procedural right to have the matter adjudicated, yet again, via the Institute's regular disciplinary system.

Keyser had no right to act as prosecutor, judge and jury, and to summarily punish Dershowitz, merely because it was obvious to Keyser that he would again be unable to get the Institute's disciplinary board to agree with his position.

Dershowitz and the MCLUF are asking for no more than that a letter be placed in Dershowitz's student file, indicating that Keyser's summary punishment and letter of reprimand are null and void, since the matter should have been prosecuted, if at all, through the Institute's duly established disciplinary mechanism, much as the first case had been.

This would end the matter. It is this which Keyser has refused to do, and which his attorneys have refused to help facilitate. Rather, the attorneys have acted as a buffer, making it difficult if not impossible for Dershowitz and me to deal directly with the Institute's administration.

MCLUF, Dershowitz and I hope that this matter might be placed on the Corporation's agenda at its next meeting.

I must add that neither Dershowitz nor MCLUF is happy with the Institute's current policy with respect to sexually explicit films being shown on campus. The version that was in effect at the time of the Dershowitz case, and the revised version in place today, are, as the Institute's own COD found, violative of academic freedom.

This substantive issue, however, is not the subject of the instant letter. The substantive issue will be raised by MCLUF at the Institute, as well as at other campuses that have adopted policies restrictive of free speech, but this will be done at a later time.

Harvey A. Silverglate

This letter really set me back on my heels. It was the personal thrust of the thing. Keyser did this egregiously and Keyser did that summarily. Keyser acted as prosecutor, judge, and jury. From the letter you'd get the impression that this Keyser guy was a pretty bad apple. But, in fact, Silverglate didn't know me from Adam. Couldn't we, at least, have talked about it first? Maybe he might have gotten to like me. I might have gotten to like him. But that was out of the question, wasn't it?

From where I sat, as soon as the matter of pornography became litigious, conversation ground to a silent (not screeching) halt. Now everything was potential fodder for the courtroom. Now the conversationalists were the lawyers. Dershowitz (Alan) was writing me. I was forbidden from answering. On March 12, 1990, Harvey Silverglate wrote me protesting Adam's not being allowed to present his case before the MIT faculty. I was forbidden from answering that letter as well. The Institute's lawyer, Jerry Weinstein, did it for me, informing Harvey Silverglate in an April 11, 1990, letter that since Adam had graduated, the reprimand had been removed from his file and the Institute considered the case closed.

In one sense Adam's violation of the pornography policy at the Institute was a great success. It produced a new pornography policy from which the prior restraint of the old policy had been expunged. It also produced what he would certainly consider the best possible pornography policy, none at all. But then there was that chilling effect, at least in my mind. From my point of view I was caught up in a battle about freedom of speech in an atmosphere in which mine, at least, was gradually suppressed to the point that I had nothing to say—not, that is, until now.

Several years after the pornography policy vanished into thin air, I was talking with a young man who had just entered MIT. Somehow the conversation turned to issues involving pornography. I told him that ten years before he came to MIT it was a matter of course to show a pornographic film in a public place at the Institute. He simply couldn't believe it. How could MIT ever have done such a thing, he wondered? It certainly wasn't showing pornography in public places now. I doubt seriously that will ever happen again now that the percentage of men and women is roughly the same. The cultural revolution, at least, was over.

But with the distance of two decades separating me from those tumultuous times, I haven't basked in the glory of a job well done. I, and a boatload of my colleagues, labored long and hard to deal with the anger that pornography produced among the increasing number of women on campus. We confronted. We met endlessly to devise and then revise a flawed policy. We sought consensus. We managed to get the Academic Council to accept a new policy that would, depending on the behavior of the community, autodestruct after three years.

But what was all of that compared with the influx of personal computers and the availability of pornography on the Internet? As a young woman from Senior House informed me recently, "We get our pornography free off the Web."

According to Gail Dines in her book *Pornland*, there are currently more than 4.2 million pornographic Web sites throughout the world with more than 420 million pages that attract some 68 million search engine requests a day. That is why, if pressed, I would credit the Internet as much as our efforts for having pushed pornography out of the public spaces at MIT and into the shadows. Has it, like our policy, disappeared? Judging from its status in 2006 as a $96 billion business worldwide, $13.33 billion of which was U.S. business, I'd say no.

On second thought, maybe pornographic movies on Registration Day are "slouch[ing] towards Bethlehem to be born" again.

8 Hacking

Although a well-known book describing the history of hacks at MIT is entitled *The Journal of the Institute for Hacks, TomFoolery, and Pranks at MIT*, the hack is anything but a prank or tomfoolery. It goes far deeper than that. It is a kind of weapon in the hands of the MIT student, but of a special kind like, for example, a tranquilizing gun. Skillful student marksmen and -women select their targets from the very top of MIT's administrative elite.

Oddly, for Lord knows how long, the only time the president ever addressed a class was when they graduated. In other words, the president never said hello to them as a group. Just goodbye. It seemed a bit unfriendly. To remedy that, when I became associate provost I started something called the President's Convocation. It was meant to be an occasion when all the freshmen and their parents gathered in Kresge Auditorium, MIT's major meeting ground, to mark the start of their careers at the Institute. MIT is notoriously ritual-free. I thought of the convocation as a rite of autumn. The first one was held in September1987.

Kresge sits in a large park just off Massachusetts Avenue. If you stand on the steps of the Institute's main entrance and look across the street, the auditorium's facade resembles the half-hidden head of a giant snake staring fiercely at the Institute in front of it. Inside that head are 1,200 seats and a large Holtkamp organ set into a loge to the right of the stage. This organ was played during the opening ceremony in 1955. The music especially commissioned for the event was Aaron Copland's "Canticle of Freedom." Some thirty-two years later, on a day in early September, the 1,200 seats of the auditorium were filled with parents and their children waiting to be addressed first by me, then by the dean of students, the head of psychiatry, the chief of the campus police, and finally the president himself, Paul E. Gray.

I was very proud of this moment. Previously there had been nothing like it. Now MIT was reaching out, saying hello to the incoming class of 1991. Only it didn't quite happen that way. I introduced Paul to the incoming class and their parents. Paul stepped up to the microphone and began to speak.

After the usual introductions, he addressed the students directly.

"In real life," he began, "technical and ethical issues are integrated."

Suddenly and mysteriously—there was no one at the keyboard—the Holtkamp organ began to play "Pop Goes the Weasel."

Paul stopped speaking. The organ stopped playing.

After a few seconds Paul went on, "The challenge is to comprehend the problem in its larger context . . ."

"Pop Goes the Weasel."

Paul stopped again. The music stopped. Paul started. "Pop Goes the Weasel" did, too, dive-bombing his speech like a mosquito in summer.

Paul's face turned red. His lower jaw jutted out, a character-istic gesture when he was really angry, which wasn't that often. He stared daggers at me.

When the convocation was over, he pulled me aside. "Did you have anything to do with this?"

"No," I protested. "Not at all."

I was shaken that the thought had even occurred to him, although I understood why. In a trial run of the event two years earlier, the president was persuaded to take part. I began that convocation wearing a suit three sizes too large. I used to fill it, but I had managed to lose weight. I tried to auction it off to the parents. I talked seriously to the parents and their children about how important it was to eat well as a college student, especially at MIT. The parents nodded approvingly.

I used myself as a model. I explained that I was living alone at the time and had perfected the art of making meals that required no washing up. One of my favorite meals was a potato baked in a microwave oven. I poked holes in a potato with a fork, set the microwave to six minutes on high, and voilà, a dishless meal.

I explained to the audience that when I mentioned this to my mother, she was horrified.

"You can't just eat one baked potato for dinner," she complained.

I told the audience that from then on I always baked two.

No wonder Paul was suspicious of me.

"If you didn't do it, find out who did," he growled.

I did. A student hanging around the lobby of Kresge with a cell phone had attracted the attention of a campus policeman. The student and several accomplices—six in all—had engineered the whole thing, with emphasis on "engineered." What the stu-dents had done was ingenious. One of them had wired the organ so that it played at the touch of a portable computer. He and his computer hid in a crawl space just beneath the stage. The problem was that from that location he couldn't hear a word Paul was saying. He needed an upstairs accomplice. The second student was stationed at the entrance to Kresge. His job was to listen to Paul's speech and signal the student under the stage when to trigger "Pop Goes the Weasel." The communication link broke down. The student under the stage had to fly blind. Unsure of what was going on just above him, he interrupted Paul once too often. What started out as a great practical joke became a rude interruption. Years later Paul told me that the really remarkable thing about this hack was its brilliant simplicity. The students had managed to play the organ with a twisted pair of wires that ran between the instrument and the basement. There was a sequel the following year. Only that one failed.

Too bad.

The day after the successful hack the students met in Paul's office. They apologized. I was present. That was the end of that. Well, almost. The whole experience triggered in me a deep interest in trying to figure out why hacking at MIT is such a rich and long-lived tradition.

The most famous set of initials at the Institute next to MIT itself isn't GPA (grade point average) or even TGIF. It is IHTFP ("I hate this fucking place"). These initials show up everywhere. You can find them embedded in the title of Brian Leibowitz's compendium of MIT hacks, *The Journal of the Institute for Hacks, TomFoolery, and Pranks at MIT.*

There are two domes that dominate the facades of MIT. The one seen from the main entrance on Massachusetts Avenue sits atop the lobby of the main building, Lobby 7. However, there is a second, bigger, and more impressive dome. It is visible from the side of MIT that faces the Charles River and looms over Killian Court where, every year, more than 2,000 graduates gather in cap and gown for the annual Commencement ceremonies. This is the Lobby 10 dome, the iconic MIT dome, the one you see in all the pictures. Because of its iconic status, it is a prime venue for student hacks. Over the years students have put everything on top of it from a phone booth to an MBTA subway car that moved back and forth to a mock-up of a Wright brothers' airplane. When students put a police car on the dome of Lobby 10 in 1994, the license plate read IHTFP. Those same letters can be found on every class ring for the past twenty years. IHTFP is always encoded somewhere on the ring, on the bezel or the shank. Sometimes it is built into the facade of the buildings in the background, sometimes in the foliage behind the beaver, but always somewhere. The reason why this is significant is that the design of the ring is the exclusive responsibility of each graduating class. If IHTFP is on the ring, it is because the graduating class wants it there.

During my years as associate provost many friends, colleagues, and associates asked me why, if students hate MIT, they don't leave it. The answer, of course, is that they don't hate it. Why, then, make such a fetish of pretending to?

Psychiatrists have a handle on that. It is called disobedient dependency, a coping mechanism meant to deal with a relationship that is both desirable and threatening—in this case, the relationship between students and faculty. The relationship is desirable for the students because, in a word, they want to be like the faculty. And the faculty is unconsciously complicit. Its leading members, whether in physics, chemistry, mathematics, or the humanities, all teach undergraduate courses. They do not send graduate student teaching assistants into the classroom as surrogates. They want to get their own hands on those students and reshape them into themselves. Think of the faculty as sorcerers and the students as sorcerers' apprentices.

What makes that apprenticeship threatening is the matter of judgment. When a faculty member is called upon to judge a student's work, that judgment is final. It is like the judgment of a sinner before the Lord. There is no place to hide. The students know the MIT faculty is for the most part world class. If the teacher says, "You are a C student," then, by God, you are a C student. That's a tough judgment to face up to, especially when you have absolute confidence in the judge. MIT students face the question "How good am I?" every semester.

This is not news. In his insightful book about the games MIT students play, *The Hidden Curriculum*, Benson Snyder made the observation forty years ago. Describing how departments compete for students by upping the ante on how hard their courses are—for an MIT student, the harder the better—he wrote:

The department's reputation, and thus its drawing power, depends in part on its reputation for being tough, by offering "the most challenging course." This creates a continual source of increasing demand on the students, *who, having internalized the university's standards and values* [italics mine], respond by demanding more and more of themselves. (pp. 82–83)

Most MIT students were in the top 5 percent of their high school classes. A poll taken before I became associate provost asked one incoming class how many of them thought they would end up in the top quarter of their class at MIT. Something like 75 percent said they would. That meant that half the incoming class was in for a rude awakening.

This rude awakening distinguishes MIT's education from that of most universities. Subjects like English, history, anthropology, and philosophy are filled with ambiguity. A poem can have dozens of interpretations, each one as good as the last. No one has a handle on truth in these fields. That is part of their attraction, that plus the fact that there are plenty of places for the student to hide. If a professor gives you a bad mark, you can always take refuge in the knowledge that he doesn't know what he's talking about. I speak from personal experience, having majored in English literature as an undergraduate at both George Washington University and Oxford.

The undergraduate experience at such institutions is, to say the least, much more liberating. As Snyder goes on to say:

Students at less selective institutions are much more likely not to take the demands of the faculty so seriously—to remain psychologically at a distance from them. This reduces the impact of the institution, but for some students it also increases freedom. (p. 83)

On the other hand, there is nothing ambiguous about mathematics, physics, or chemistry. The professors know what they are talking about. Otherwise they wouldn't be professors. A student's answers to a problem set are either right or wrong. Being an undergraduate at MIT is like auditioning for a major symphony orchestra. You either cut it or you don't. No shades of gray. No wonder the students have developed a hacking culture.

A practical joke is a joke you play on someone. The point is to make the butt of the joke look silly. That is precisely what an MIT hack is, a practical joke played on the Institute to make it look silly. It is meant to debunk the Institute's authority. MIT hacks, unlike hacks at other institutions, have a strong engineering component. They parody engineering by impersonating it and then pulling the rug out from under it. MIT hackers typically don't throw pies or put brassieres on statues of founding fathers. Rather, they make large objects like a police car or a telephone booth or a model of a Wright brothers' airplane or a facsimile of an MBTA subway car appear in inaccessible places like the flat space atop the dome of Lobby 10.

In 1994 they replaced the pompous, chiseled wisdom on the frieze around the 100-foot-high rotunda in Lobby 7 with something sillier and more relevant. They did this so cleverly that it was several days before anyone noticed that the original "Established for advancement and development of science and its application to industry arts agriculture and commerce" had been changed to "Established for advancement and development of science and its application to industry arts entertainment and hacking." A special team of trained rappelers had to be called in to dismantle the hack, the hackers having left instructions on how to take it apart.

During my time as associate provost, I was often asked to give talks at MIT clubs throughout the country. These are clubs whose members are MIT alumni who want to maintain a connection. Not surprisingly, at least to me, the topic they most often wanted me to talk about was MIT hacks. Why not? Most MIT alumni identified with the hackers when they were students. Sometime in the mid-1990s I gave a hack talk to the MIT club in Chicago. It was a walk down hack-memory lane starting with the 1925 hack when students took apart a Model T Ford and then put it back together on the roof of East Campus, one of the MIT dormitories. After the talk several of the members came up to me to ask questions and to sharpen my picture of one hack or another. A young woman who had been standing at the fringes of the group edged her way to the center and said, "If you think carving those friezes into Styrofoam boards so they looked like the originals was easy, think again." Then she disappeared.

Who was that masked woman?

During the 1980s President Gray and his wife, Priscilla, gave garden parties for the parents of incoming freshmen. The president's garden was filled with neophytes and their parents. Several Senior House students took this as an opportunity to be ostentatiously disobedient. They would dress as grungily as possible. Then they would scale the wall separating the Senior House courtyard from the president's garden and mingle with the well-dressed, well-scrubbed guests, scarfing crabmeat sandwiches as if they were auditioning for the part of John Belushi in a remake of *Animal House*. The more outrageous the behavior, the better. Some of the more inventive students would dress up as characters from *The Rocky Horror Picture Show*. Most, however, did not, attempting to épater les bourgeois by the mere outrageousness of their presence. More often than not, the students would empty a bottle of detergent into the garden fountain in order to intensify their nuisance value, all the while setting an example for the incoming freshmen who saw them "getting away with it."

The superficial motive behind such "disobedience" was to embarrass those in authority: the president, his spouse, the various deans and housemasters who showed up for the occasion. The crashers were declaring their independence from the Institute and all its folderol. The deeper motive was to distance themselves from an Institute whose judgments—which they could not help but accept—were more often than not painful. Sound familiar? It ought to, to anyone who has had teenage children.

This kind of public rudeness is not a hack, even though it stems from the same psychological impulse. There is, after all, more than one way to skin a cat. Unlike extreme kinds of misbehavior, like crashing the president's garden party, the hack is an institutionally acceptable form of disobedience that has evolved at MIT for close to a century. (One of the earliest if not the first hack was that Model T on the roof of East Campus in 1925.)

Hacks are easily distinguished from other acts of disobedient dependency by three properties. They are (1) technologically sophisticated, (2) anonymous, (3) benign. They are technologically sophisticated because they need to parody an MIT education. They are anonymous because were they otherwise, the Institute might be forced, for safety reasons, to do something about them. They are benign because their goal is not to inflict pain, but to cope with pain inflicted. They do this by making fun of the Institute, not by damaging it. It has become a mark of pride to perform a complicated hack that has a completely erasable footprint.

One day I received a call from a friend in Audio Visual Services. He knew my interest in hacks. He was taping a lecture in MIT's largest lecture hall, 10-250 (note the use of a number, not a name). "You ought to get down here right away," he said. "I think you'll find it interesting."

I arrived at the hall in time to see the lecturer, Sigurdur Helgason, approach the rightmost blackboard. It was electronically controlled. When the blackboard was filled with formulas, the lecturer would touch a button that moved it up, revealing a fresh board underneath. If the lecturer wanted to refer to a formula on the higher board, the touch of a button brought it back down.

As Sigurdur approached the board to write an equation on it—this was a calculus class—the blackboard mysteriously floated up out of reach. Sigurdur didn't bat an eye. He moved to the central blackboard. The same thing happened: just as he reached up to write, the blackboard rose out of his reach. Sigurdur turned to the leftmost blackboard, the only one that had to be raised and lowered manually. Without missing a beat, he said, "From this point on I will conduct the class from this board. The other two are highly unreliable."

After class, my friend unscrewed the metal plate on the control panel. Inside he found a radio receiver taken from the innards of a remote-controlled racing car of the kind sold at Radio Shack. Using removable alligator clips, the hacker had attached it to the electrical terminals of the elevating mechanism. The perpetrator must have been seated in the first three rows to stay within range of the receiver. He (or she) would have been using a joystick to raise and lower the blackboards, the joystick that under normal circumstances made a toy racing car go left or right. The clips were cushioned with a wad of scrunched-up paper towels. All my friend needed to do was remove the paper batting, unclip the receiver, and screw the plate back on.

This hack was exemplary. It was technologically smart, anonymous, and benign. No one or thing was damaged, except, perhaps, the dignity of the Institute. The Institute would get over it. The hack also illustrates the social contract that MIT and its students enter into. Keep it anonymous, harmless, and fun and MIT looks the other way.

The importance of these gestures is reflected in this reminiscence of an MIT alumnus to be found on a class of 1982 Web site under the rubric "Memories of MIT":

Exploring the space between the inner and outer domes above Lobby 7. Watching as a friend took over the black boards in 10-250 via a wireless device. Finding a large vacuum-tube device hackers from long ago left behind.

The adversarial nature of the student-faculty relationship at the Institute will never completely disappear any more than it will disappear between parents and their teenage children. It won't matter how supportive student services are or how solicitous the staff might be or how accessible the faculty makes itself or how much our culture might change the character of the typical MIT student. Hacks and the living groups will always be to the Institute what sunglasses are to the sun: a form of protection that makes it possible to cope with intense light.

9   Role Compliance

For as long as I have been at MIT the administrative pulse of the place has beat in the life of its committees. Not everyone at MIT serves on committees. In fact, not everyone should. Certainly junior faculty members, who are trying to fight their way up the tenure ladder, need to keep their noses to the grindstone. (I think it is fun to mix metaphors.)

Roughly 20 percent of the faculty are civic minded enough to volunteer for committee assignments. Serving on committees is how people get to know one another in a university where the occasions for collegiality are few and far between. It is also where the real business of the Institute gets done—at least it was when I was associate provost.

The committees took their charges seriously. The rest of the faculty trusted them to do just that. And God help the administration that made decisions outside the committee culture. In January 1988 the administration closed down the Department of Applied Biological Sciences. It did so without the advice and consent of a faculty committee. All hell broke loose. Graduate students in the doomed department circulated a petition with over a hundred names, deploring the administration's motivation. At a faculty meeting in February 1988, the faculty excoriated the administration for the high-handed (read "no committee involvement") fashion in which it went about disbanding a department. The doomed department head, Gerald Wogan, expressed "disappointment with the surprising process."

Just one month later, at the March 1988 faculty meeting, an Ad Hoc Committee on Reorganization and Closing of Academic Units was formed. Talk about closing the barn door after the horse has bolted. The ostensible reason for the committee was to lay down guidelines for future closings. The real point of the committee was to slap a faculty committee ruler across the administration's open palm. This it did in part by including the following paragraph in its final report:

It is the view of this committee, and we believe of the faculty at large, that a key to the success of the Institute has been the maintenance of a system of shared governance. Few of the MIT faculty see themselves in an employee-employer relationship with the Administration. Rather, most feel that the Administration and faculty share a joint responsibility for sustaining the excellence of the Institute. They expect that, when important choices arise about mission or internal organization, they will naturally be involved in the process leading up to decisions and in the planning of implementation.

Shortly after news of the administration's intentions was made public, John Deutch, my boss, asked me how serious things were. Not very, I said. I told him I thought it would all blow over quickly. I also thought Ronald Reagan would never be president. So much for my political perspicacity. As a result of the Applied Biological Sciences fiasco, any hope of John's becoming MIT's next president were dashed. Hell hath no fury like the MIT faculty scorned. Commenting on the criticism, Paul Gray (a former MIT chancellor, president, and chairman of the Corporation) said, "There's no good way to shut anything down at MIT."

When John said to me some twenty years after the fact "I set you up, didn't I?" he was referring to his decision to put me in the line of pornographic fire. He could just as easily have been referring to the MIT Committee on Sexual Harassment. I was to fill it, staff it and chair it. The proximate cause was a complaint by thirteen graduate students from the School of Science, all women. They were angry at what they perceived to be MIT's unwillingness or inability or both to deal with sexual harassment. There was, they held, no clear Institute-wide definition of sexual harassment and no clear procedure for bringing charges that protected the complainant. They told John so in a visit to his office early in 1989. Afterward he called me in and said, "When thirteen women from the same school have the same complaint, you pay attention."

The first meeting of the committee took place on December 7, 1989. John insisted on a final report by March 1990. He was obviously in a hurry. This was the committee's charge:

Within the context of the Institute's policy on harassment, consider possible modifications which would strengthen the policy's effectiveness in reducing instances of sexual harassment and in handling instances when they arise.

Establish the outlines of a community-wide program of prevention and support designed to produce an atmosphere in which sexual harassment is universally regarded as unacceptable behavior, and in which the institutional mechanisms for treating incidents of sexual harassment are well understood.

Propose actions to heighten community awareness among academic, administrative and research supervisors at all levels such that the occurrence of instances of sexual harassment are (sic) radically decreased, if not completely eliminated.

Propose steps to reduce the occurrence of instances of sexual harassment in campus residences and MIT living groups and to facilitate prompt and fair redress for such instances.

Paul Gray had doubled the number of women at MIT between 1980 and 1985. It took just one class cycle, another four years, to bring on a perfect storm of cultural upheaval. In 1987 Adam Dershowitz announced his intention to show *Deep Throat* in Talbot Lounge. In 1989 John Deutch met with the thirteen graduate women in the School of Science. The MIT Committee on Sexual Harassment was a direct outcome of that visit. It was made up of seventeen members of the community including a dean, a department head, three faculty members, six members of the administration, two ombudspeople, two students (one undergraduate, the other a graduate), one postdoc, and me. Every corner of the Institute was covered.

Chairing this committee was the hardest assignment I had ever handled. The reason was the anger. At every meeting it hung over the conference table like smog over LA. That anger stemmed mainly from the students. They had, I suspected, either experienced harassment first hand or had close friends who had. I dreaded the meetings. The simplest issues took on a symbolic significance that went way beyond the surface of things. I never knew when someone might go ballistic.

As it happened, I was in psychotherapy at the time. I have always thought that MIT should have put my psychiatrist on its payroll.

One morning I received a call from one of the high-level administrators on the committee. She told me that one of the student members wanted to meet with me and wanted the administrator to come along. I agreed and a date for the meeting was set. The meeting took place in my office. I cannot for the life of me remember what the meeting was about. Here is what I do remember.

The next day the student passed me in the corridor outside my office. I said hello.

She stopped and said, "What you did yesterday was despicable."

I felt as if I had been hit in the stomach with a sledgehammer. I was primed for it, I suppose, a paranoid just waiting for the other hobnailed boot to drop.

"What did I do?" I stammered.

"If you don't know, then there's no point in my telling you," was the response. The student turned and walked away.

I saw the whole committee stack of cards tumbling down. I had been rolling the rock of sexual harassment up a mountain and now it was about to roll back on me.

I rushed back into my office and called the senior administrator who had accompanied the student. I told her what had just happened. "What did I do?" I pleaded. "It must have been something I said. What did I say?"

"I haven't a clue," the administrator replied.

Thank goodness for my therapist. I had seen the student and the administrator in my office on a Monday morning. The encounter with the student in the corridor happened on Tuesday. The next meeting of the committee wasn't until Friday and, thankfully, I had an appointment to see my shrink on Wednesday. It was shaping up to be a full week.

I told my shrink what had happened.

He listened intently, as he always did. When I was finished, he nodded. "Have you ever heard of role compliance?" he asked.

I shook my head.

"There are some people who have a theory of what the world is like and how the people in it act toward them. They assign a role to you. Then they act toward you in such a way as to make their theory come true. If you cooperate, you are role compliant."

"So . . . " I said, leaning forward in my chair.

"So," he answered, "be careful."

It was the best of advice.

When I returned to my office the next day, the Thursday before the next committee meeting, I discovered that the student had made an appointment to see me that afternoon. She was coming alone.

She didn't mince words. "I think my anger is getting in the way of the work of the committee. I've come to ask if you think I should resign."

I remembered my shrink's words: be careful. If this was role compliance at work, then a likely scenario was that I would agree that her anger did have a deleterious effect and that I thought resigning would be a great help to the committee and a tremendous relief for me. I wasn't about to sink into that morass.

I said to myself, "Resign? No, I don't want you to resign. I want you to throw yourself under a subway car."

I said to her, "Resign? No, I don't want you to resign. I want you to stay on the committee and continue to work with it. Your voice is very important."

For the rest of the hour she came at me sixty ways from Sunday. Each time I rebuffed the attack. I kept uppermost in my mind the image of our meeting beginning the next morning with my visitor announcing to the committee that the chairman—that's me—had asked her to resign and that she was doing so as of now. I saw a grand and huffy exit from the committee room followed by headlines in the student paper: Keyser Forces

Student Rep to Exit Harassment Committee. The first line of the imaginary article began, "Ms. X, an active mover and shaker in the fight against sexual harassment at the Institute, has been ousted from the very committee she helped bring into being by its chairman, associate provost Samuel Jay Mud."

That image was enough to prevent me from falling down that particular rabbit hole. My shrink's heads-up on role compliance saved me from making a fool of myself not only in this instance but in any number of situations down the road.

As it was, the student rep stuck it out. The committee lumbered along, completing its work in March 1990 as John Deutch had asked. Much to my astonishment, every single member of the committee signed the final report.

There is, however, a deeper significance to these events. If someone were to ask me to boil down my tenure as a complaint-handling associate provost—that is pretty much what the last five years of my job amounted to—into two words, those words would be "role" and "compliance." In retrospect I can't think of a single instance where I found myself dealing with a conflict involving students, faculty, and staff or some combination of the three that didn't involve role compliance on the part of the major players.

A July 11, 2010, *Boston Globe* article described human subject experiments intended to explore the effect of facts on strongly held views. The experimenters claimed that if people hold strong views about some topic—say, that everyone on welfare is a cheat—and if those subjects are shown facts that contradict that view—say, that .01 percent of those on welfare have been shown to cheat—their advocacy of the welfare-recipients-are-cheaters worldview becomes, if anything, more strongly held.

I didn't follow up the references in this article because—well, because they seemed perfectly obvious to me from my experience as associate provost for dispute resolution. (That should have been my title.) The views that people hold are part and parcel of their sense of their own personality. An attack on those views is a threat to their view of themselves. That is just another way of saying "role compliance." To any administrator or parent who has had the patience to read this far, I would repeat the wise words of my erstwhile therapist: be careful.

10 "Don't Tell Me What to Do"

In early November 1989 Jake Jacoby, the chair of the faculty at the time, visited with members of the MIT Undergraduate Association. The issue was MIT's pornography policy. His was a reaching-out exercise. Jake wanted to engage the students in a conversation about pornography in general, hoping that by doing so he could muster student support for "an abuse and degradation free community." On November 16 Jake wrote a memorandum to file, an elaborate note to himself about the meeting. It ended:

Finally, it occurred to me after the meeting was over that a major thread of discussion was not so much "I have a right to see pornography and it's O.K. for us to do this." Really what several undergraduates were saying was, "Don't tell me what to do."

That warning, contained in six stark, Anglo-Saxon syllables, pretty much sums up the dominant MIT student culture that I came in contact with during my seven years as housemaster at Senior House. It isn't too hard to see where it comes from. If you squint your eyes a bit, you can almost see truculent teenagers saying precisely that to their holding-the-purse-strings parents, or maybe, if they are not actually saying it, wishing they could.

The students had devoted so much of their adolescent years to preparing themselves to be accepted by MIT that they hadn't managed the equally important task of separating from home. That task comes to the fore once the students arrive on campus. And then it arrives with a vengeance.

MIT, like many universities in America, sits in what is called "in loco parentis," in place of parents. MIT cannot sidestep this role. It guarantees its undergraduates housing for the four years that they are in attendance. That brings with it a lot of responsibility and a lot of headaches. There are rooms to be readied, dining halls to be equipped, dining plans to be designed, safe rides from one part of campus to another to be supplied, medical (including psychiatric) services to be provided, and that's just the beginning. In other words, MIT has taken on the task of providing students with all the comforts and safety nets of home. It's a tough job. It's also a job that the students need done while simultaneously resenting that they need it.

In 1993, on November 1 to be exact, just hours after it appeared in their mailboxes, several Senior House students burned a document called "Dealing with Harassment at MIT." This was the document that came out of the findings of the Committee on Sexual Harassment that I had chaired from December 1989 through March 1990. It took three years to put it together after countless hours of discussion, debate, and talking it through with various Institute students, staff, and faculty.

The *Tech* of November 2, 1993, featured pictures of students throwing the guides onto a bonfire. I had been out of Senior House for five years by then. But when I saw the photographs, my old anger came out of hiding. It surprised me. I was hoping it had pulled up stakes and decamped. Apparently not. The pictures made me think of the Nazi book burnings in Munich. These students haven't a clue, I thought. The spectacle of burning a book in an MIT dormitory, any book, with all of the ugly resonances that dredged up, was lost on them. What was worse, I thought, was that if you were to try to explain it, they would reply with their own version of "Don't tell me what to do." (Three years later the students burned the Senior House constitution. At least they were eclectic about their bonfires.)

One week after the document appeared Adam Dershowitz wrote this, in a guest column in the *Tech*:

> When a group of students chose to voice its opinion about the success of the many hours of work and the tens of thousands of dollars that must have been invested in this document by burning it, did the action "create an intimidating, hostile, or offensive educational, work, or living environment?" If so it was therefore harassment! If I had put that much work into something I would have been offended at having it burned, but then again, I would never admit to writing anything as silly as this guide, and in this case no one has put his name to the guide.

As one of those who had put "many hours of work" into the document, I didn't feel harassed, just angry at the insensitivity of the book burners. A psychiatrist friend of mine recently suggested to me that mankind's troubles emanate not from a well of sexuality but from an arsenal of aggression. Certainly, that seemed to be true with respect to the harassment conflict.

These students were supposed to be the best that America had to offer. They were the next generation of scientists and engineers. What exactly was it that had upset them? The offending paragraph was on page 18 of "Dealing with Harassment at MIT." It said:

> Freedom of expression is essential to the mission of a university. So is freedom from unreasonable and disruptive offense. Members of this educational community are encouraged to avoid putting these essential elements of our university to a balancing test.

The intent of the paragraph was to say that while you have the right to call your next-door neighbor "a fucking idiot," please think twice before you do. That paragraph could have been put into one simple sentence: be civil to one another. It didn't tell anyone what to do. But it led to a book burning in Senior House and articles in the *Tech* (November 9, 1993) with headlines like "MIT Harassment Handbook Constitutes Fascist Policy."

It certainly didn't have to be that way. In 2007 my wife, Nancy, and I visited Bhutan, a tiny kingdom north of India and south of China. It is the most civil society I have ever encountered, and certainly the most serene. One day we told our guide we wanted to buy a metal Bhutanese Buddha to take home with us as a memento of our visit. He said the Bhutanese Buddhas were always made of clay or wood. Nonetheless, we found a metal Buddha that the shopkeeper swore on a stack of sutras was Bhutanese. When we showed it to our guide, he didn't say, "Well, they certainly saw you coming, Dumbo!" He said, quite simply, "If it pleases you, I am glad." When was the last time somebody at MIT who disagreed with my position on pornography, harassment, or apartheid said, "Well, if it pleases you to think that, I am glad"?

One has to look behind book-burning behavior to understand it. But one doesn't have to look very far. It has "Don't tell me what to do" written all over it. And that, in turn, stems from "I am a grown-up and can make my own decisions, Daddy." Only it is not the real daddy they are addressing. It is the Institute playing daddy—that is, the Institute in loco parentis. And, frankly, having to deal with all that acting out because it wasn't settled before the students came to MIT is a pain in the ass.

While I was writing this book, I met with a Senior House resident to get an up-to-date sense of the culture there in 2010. She was kind enough to visit me in my office. I learned that she was an officer of the house and that from her perspective Senior House and she were a marriage made in living-group heaven.

Going back in my mind to the eighties, I remembered students describing the close ties they formed with their living groups. If two alumni were to meet halfway around the world, at a conference, say, they identified themselves, not as MIT alums, but as living group alums: "I'm Baker House," "I'm Next House," "I'm MacGregor." I understood this. Where they lived was, as I've said, safe harbor from the academic storm of MIT.

So I asked my visitor, "Do you feel a loyalty to MIT?"

"Yes," she said firmly.

That was a real change in the weather. Things are different, I thought. But then she went on.

"But in more recent situations where it's very easy to say that MIT is always wrong, no. Several people, I would say, have a loyalty to Senior House over MIT or to their dorms in general over MIT."

I asked her what those recent situations were. A major one had to do with dining regulations, a complicated confluence of MIT providing food services at certain hours and students being told what they had to do if they wanted to avail themselves of those services. That the issue of right and wrong involved food was not a surprise.

Around 1985 my mother finally relented and agreed to move into an assisted living facility near me. She was eighty years old at the time and had been living alone in another city. No sooner had she moved in than she began to complain, even though the building was clean, her rooms airy, and the amenities acceptable. "The food," she said, "is terrible." I went to lunch to check it out. It turned out to be pretty good.

It took me a while to figure out that food was her barometer of independence. If she allowed herself to like the food, then she became dependent on the facility. That was threatening. That was a loss of control.

My visitor's complaint about the dining service was a horse of the same color. My visitor and her friends both in Senior House and across campus, the ones who were fighting the dining hall battle, were fighting their own war of independence. They no more wanted to be dependent on their surrogate parent—the one that stood in loco parentis—than they did on their real parents.

I asked my visitor about drugs. Sure enough, two years before our conversation four students were hospitalized after taking an unhealthy combination of alcohol and GHB (known as the date rape drug) at Steer Roast. They were not Senior House students. Apparently, they had managed to wriggle in from outside. News of Steer Roast gets around.

"What about pornography?" I asked. "Do you still do pornography?"

She nodded.

"The Virgin Killer award?"

She nodded again.

"My argument against pornography when I was housemaster was that no one should interfere with your right to watch it, but it wasn't OK to pay for it because that involved supporting a dehumanizing industry."

She thought for a moment and then said, "That's a reasonable argument. Only it doesn't hold anymore. We get our pornography free off the Web."

In a nutshell, being in loco parentis is the soft underbelly of MIT and, I suppose, of every university or college that provides its students with a place to live. The situation the students find themselves in is simply too much like home. And all the unresolved issues, all the adolescent baggage they carry with them along with their real baggage, becomes the burden of the institution.

Students work out their separation issues in a wide variety of ways including protests against apartheid, for free speech, against dining regulations, for lower tuition, you name it. This isn't to say that there isn't substance to their protests. But it *is* to say that the issue is never as simple as Apartheid Bad, Freedom of Speech Good. The specific protest is simply the tip of the iceberg and as with all icebergs, nine-tenths of what's really there is below the surface. This is part of what makes managing protest so difficult.

Does the faculty have a role in all this? Yes, they do. I always thought it was odd that MIT faculty members thought it appropriate to pony up for the court costs of student protesters when, for one reason or another, they were forced to go to court, something that happened a number of times during my tenure as associate provost. What was that all about? If the students were adults, then they ought to be ready to suffer the consequences of their actions, even if that meant coughing up $50 in court costs. But there was always a group of faculty members willing to dig down and come up with the money. Wasn't that infantilizing the students?

Well, not to put too fine a point on it, it was. The faculty is genuinely conflicted about being in loco parentis. Many faculty members believe that is precisely where they ought to be. They view themselves as having a special relationship to their students. They will describe it in a variety of terms. They will say that we are all part of the same community and we need to protect and support one another however we can. In that last sentence substitute "family" for "community" and you get the idea.

These faculty members think it's perfectly fine for a pair of neighborhood kids caught with a keg of nitrous oxide to be taken to the Cambridge police while it makes perfect sense for a pair of MIT students caught with the same sort of keg to be taken to the campus police. Why? Because the MIT students are family. It's worth taking a closer look at that notion, especially when the issue is not drugs but social protest.

11 Apartheid

The business of having to deal with people who never see you but instead see their theory of you was at the heart of many if not most of the conflicts I dealt with. That is undoubtedly why, for most of my senior administrative life, I had the impression that I was a character in a play written by someone else. Who knew that psychiatrists had plastered a label on it? One of the major conflicts of my Institute life had "role compliance" tattooed across its forehead.

On Wednesday, November 20, 1985, a motion was introduced into the regular monthly meeting of the MIT faculty. The gist of the motion was to ask the MIT Corporation to divest from companies doing business in or with South Africa. At the time of the motion MIT's policy had been to invest in corporations abiding by the so-called Sullivan Principles, named after a preacher, Leon Sullivan. (He later renounced them, having come to believe that they were not doing the job.) The principles were essentially a corporate code of conduct. They espoused nonsegregation in the workplace, equal pay, programs to train blacks for management positions, that sort of thing.

On one side of the faculty debate were those who argued that MIT's investments were morally reprehensible, tantamount to investments in apartheid. Those on the other side argued that businesses adhering to the Sullivan Principles in South Africa were a positive force that would ultimately work against apartheid, that divestment would amount to letting the air out of the antiapartheid balloon.

The final vote would come up a month later, on December 18, 1985. I would have a month to stew about it. My inclination was to vote for divestment. My hesitation was that the president, Paul Gray, and the Corporation were against divesting. They supported MIT's Sullivan Principles stance. As of the November meeting MIT had $150 million invested in companies that were to some degree in accord with those principles. The funds involved were by no means trivial. They amounted, at the time, to something like 18 percent of MIT's total endowment. Although the figure was disputed, the treasurer estimated that divesting would have cost MIT $10 million had it divested six years earlier.

I worried how I could in good faith be a member of the administration and not support divestment. If I voted against divestment, I would be going against my conscience. If I voted for, I would be going against the administration that I was a part of. I decided to tell Paul how I intended to vote and to offer my resignation. About a week before the vote I made an appointment to see him. I had been associate provost for five months by this time. When I explained how I felt, I asked if he wanted me to resign. He looked at me as though I'd asked him if he wanted me to short-sheet the beds in the MIT infirmary. Obviously I hadn't quite got the hang of being an administrator in MIT's Mahogany Row, the section of the Institute that housed at that time the offices of the president, the provost, the treasurer, the senior vice president, the vice president and secretary of the Corporation, the vice president for research, the dean for undergraduate education, and me. Toeing a particular line was not part of the deal.

On December 18, 1985, the faculty voted 131 to 40 to take every step possible to end apartheid, "including the divestment of holdings in those firms doing business in or lending to South Africa." I was one of the 131. The faculty vote was the calm before the storm. In 1984 a group of students had formed an organization called the Coalition against Apartheid (CAA). They planned and executed a number of demonstrations. One of them involved a reception for Dr. Nthato Motlana, chairman of the Soweto Committee of Ten. Dr. Motlana spoke at an MIT-sponsored Institute-wide colloquium on November 8, 1985. At a reception held afterward in McCormick Hall, an MIT all-women's dormitory, ten CAA members marched in carrying antiapartheid banners. The student newspaper, the *Tech* (November 8, 1985), quoted the demonstrators: "This whole thing is just organized to take away from the mass movement"; MIT's colloquium was simply a feint designed to "talk the movement to death."

Here was role compliance in spades. No matter what MIT did, the protesters saw it as sinister. They viewed MIT as an accomplice in one of the world's most abominable oppressions. Nothing MIT did short of divestment would change that view. Indeed, even if MIT had divested, I suspect it would still have been seen as a sinister body forced for once to do the right thing.

The matter came to a head a few months later. On February 26, 1986, the CAA submitted a request to Steve Immerman, then director of operations for the West Plaza area, seeking permission to build a shantytown on the Kresge Oval.

The Oval is a large green across the street from MIT's main entrance. It is one of the Institute's central and most accessible meeting places. Like an inland peninsula, it is surrounded on

three sides by buildings. On the north side is the Stratton Building, which houses the Student Center. On the south side is the
MIT chapel. To the west is Kresge Auditorium. Traffic through
the Oval is always heavy, with students and faculty crossing
Massachusetts Avenue to get to the long row of dormitories
beyond Kresge, the athletic fields behind, or the Student Center.
The CAA chose well.

They also behaved well; at least it started out that way. They
asked for permission to build the shanties. They even specified
a date when the shanties would come down: March 13, 1986.
The end date was not accidental. On March 6 there would be
a meeting of the Executive Committee of the Corporation, the
heart of MIT power. The following day the Corporation itself
would meet. The CAA wanted to make sure the Corporation was
listening. On March 12 the Undergraduate Association planned
a referendum on divestment. The idea was to end the shanty
demonstration the day after that.

That was the good news. The bad news was that while the
students were negotiating with Immerman, they withdrew their
application. The "negotiations" were ostensibly around safety
concerns. The shanties must not be higher than one story. There
could be no open fires. The fire lanes must remain clear. This was
a nonstarter. The administration was telling the students what
they could and couldn't do. From the administration's point
of view, safety was the paramount concern. From the students'
point of view, the issue was freedom from authority. One of the
CAA representatives was quoted in the *Tech* (March 15, 1986) as
saying that the shanties would go up "no matter what Gray said.
There really aren't any options for the administration."

That response had all the markings of the beginning of the
end, beginning with the reference to the president as "Gray,"

not "the president" or "President Gray" or "Dr. Gray." That was the first indication to me that things were going awry, a bit like the swelling in the groin before the plague sets in. When I read it, a sense of dread came over me. I was remembering the 1968 Columbia University protest when a group of students occupied several campus buildings. The day before the takeover, April 22, the leader of the white student faction, Mark Rudd, wrote a letter to the president of Columbia University, Grayson Kirk. The occasion of the letter was a comment Kirk had made in a speech in Charlottesville, Virginia, on April 12:

Our young people, in disturbing numbers, appear to reject all forms of authority, from whatever source derived, and they have taken refuge in a turbulent and inchoate nihilism whose sole objectives are destruction. I know of no time in our history when the gap between the generations has been wider or more potentially dangerous.

Rudd's letter was an angry and articulate complaint, ranging over the university's involvement in the Vietnam War, its expansion into predominantly black neighborhoods in Morningside Heights and Harlem, and even its educational curriculum—designed, as Rudd saw it, to prepare students to be servants of "corporate capitalism." As I recall from reading about the revolt, Rudd had no trouble writing the letter. However, the salutation gave him pause. What should it be? Dear President Kirk? Dear Mr. Kirk? Motherfucker?—he actually closed with the latter. In the end he chose just the right salutation to get as deeply as possible under President Kirk's skin without actually piercing it. In a masterstroke of acupunctural invective, he began his letter, "Dear Grayson."

Now, at MIT, sixteen years later, the same needling of authority was in the air. It was a foregone conclusion as far as I was concerned that once the shanties went up, they would come down with a great noise. Up they went on Sunday, March 2, 1986. They became an instant focal point of antiapartheid activity. A march on the president's house on Thursday, March 6, drew 100 protesters to the sidewalk outside the president's house. The next day the protests escalated. Again over 100 protesters stood outside the president's house. The occasion was the meeting of the MIT Corporation on the inside. The protesters wanted to address the full meeting of the Corporation. Paul Gray responded that he had no intention of inviting them in. There were shouts of "Paul Gray. You can't hide. We know you're on apartheid's side." The protesters moved to the Sloan Building, where the Corporation meeting was continuing. There were scuffles in the elevator to block them. The stairwells were not blocked. The students made their way to the sixth floor and pounded on doors, trying to find a way to address the Corporation on apartheid, invited or not. Afterward there were complaints of police brutality.

The tension on campus was ratcheting up. On the same day that the protesters were tracking the Corporation in an attempt to talk to them, Constantine Simonides, the vice president and secretary of the Corporation, received a petition with 144 signatures supporting the antiapartheid movement and the right of students to protest but objecting to the shanties on Kresge Oval. The administration was being maneuvered into an untenable position between the rock of student protest and the hard place of protest backlash. This position was and has always been an impossible one for universities.

Once a protest movement succeeds in making the university a part of the problem, the institution is doomed to lose. The administration is supposed to be the neutral party, allowing a fair hearing for all sides. But it can't be in both places at the same time, a neutral and a participant. Any attempt to impose limits on either of the opposing parties, for whatever reason, is tantamount to bias, partisanship, and a guilty plea. That is certainly what happened at MIT. The protesters succeeded in pushing the administration into saying "Enough is enough." The rest was helpless history.

From the day the shanties went up, MIT posted two officers around the clock to avoid student-on-student imbroglios. The precaution wasn't in vain. At 3 a.m. on the day of the Corporation meeting, a number of people suddenly appeared on the Oval and made their way toward the shanties. When the campus police stepped out of the shadows, the group backed off. It was a menacing event that colored the thinking of the administration from that point on. It certainly colored mine.

The administration was nervous. And when the administration is nervous, it holds meetings. This occasion was no exception. Numerous meetings were held, though none with members of the CAA. By this time the line had been drawn. It had turned into a "them vs. us" situation with "them" being the CAA leadership. The faculty was not involved—did not, in fact, involve itself. Nor did the administration make an effort to involve the faculty. One of the few conduits between the administration and the students was the then president of the Undergraduate Association. He was out of town. It isn't clear to me that his presence would have helped much. As I said, a line had been drawn. It was hard for things to have been otherwise, what with the students surrounding Paul Gray's house and with Paul walking across campus with a police escort. The central question had become not whether the shanties should come down, but when. The rights and wrongs of apartheid now took a back seat to a game of chicken.

The decision to dismantle was made on the afternoon of Thursday, March 13, at a T-group (T for "tactical") meeting convened by Constantine. Such meetings were an outgrowth of past crises on campus. The chief actors were administrators. Significantly, no students were present. In other words, "them vs. us" was now conventional wisdom. The three senior officers present were Constantine, Bill Dickson (the senior vice president and the man on whom fell the brunt of the actual demolition), and me. It gives me pause to think that two of the three of us are now dead.

Constantine summarized the argument for taking the shanties down. First, the Oval belonged to everyone, not just the CAA. Second, there was a real possibility of a clash with students who wanted the shanties out of there. The argument against taking them down was simple: dismantling the shanties looked an awful lot like dismantling dissent. I argued that there wasn't any rush. Sooner or later the shanties would come down of their own accord. After all, the end of the term was only six weeks away.

So what was the rush? In a nutshell, it was the threat of violence. At the T-group meeting the Campus Police representative reported that three carloads of young men had driven up to the Oval, gotten out, and given the protesters a fascist salute.

Up to then I had been strongly against the shanties' coming down. Now the threat of violence was real. I could no longer see the conflict as a game. Now it wasn't simply students pushing the buttons of those in loco parentis. Now there was the threat of violence, student against student or student against townie. (It was never clear who the three carloads of young men were.) To put it bluntly, I was worried that the protesters might get the shit knocked out of them. They were very good when it came to fighting the likes of me, but I wasn't at all convinced that they were good at fighting the likes of themselves. The debate was over. The shanties would come down. I doubt the decision would have been much different even if I hadn't wavered. It doesn't really matter, of course, except to me.

The T-group took a leaf out of Macbeth's book: "If it were done when 'tis done, then 'twere well it were done quickly." The shanties would come down, and they would come down the very next morning. At 8 o'clock. Part of the reason for the haste was a leaflet distributed by the CAA, announcing that 58 percent of the undergraduate student body had voted for divestment and that the graduate student body had voted for divestment by a 4 to 1 margin.

Given this strong student support, the organizers declared in the leaflet, entitled "Shantytown Update," that they had decided to maintain their "vigil at Alexandra Township on the Kresge Oval as a stark reminder to the MIT Corporation that the students here will be persistent in the divestment struggle." They envisioned the township as a place where students might come to "feel comfortable" as they learned more about the antiapartheid movement. They planned activities consistent with that goal: "Toward this end, some of the more artistically inclined members of the Coalition are sponsoring a tie-dye workshop this Saturday afternoon."

I was struck by the wording of this. "Some of the more artistically inclined members of the Coalition" sounded like an apology. It was as if the writers were saying, "We have no idea where these tie-dyers are coming from. After all, this is an engineering school, not a playground. But we are a democratically organized Coalition and if some of our members want to tie-dye against apartheid, so be it."

How, I argued, could we close down a shantytown that was intending to promote tie-dying as a protest activity? But close it down we did.

At 5:15 p.m. almost everyone present indicated agreement with the decision to dismantle. Bill Dickson left the room to convey the news to Paul Gray, who was in Japan. When Bill returned, the meeting turned to specifics. It was decided that the campus police would talk quietly to the students, letting them know what was in the cards. Then the Physical Plant workers would begin to take the shanties down. If the students at the shanties objected, a trespass warning would be given. The next item on the T-group's agenda was, who would be the messenger? Constantine offered to do it. That was ruled out. After all, he was a member and an officer of the Corporation and therefore one of the people directly in the students' line of fire. I was never a candidate. Too wishy-washy. Bill Dickson agreed to do the deed. He was senior officer for operations. The people doing the dirty work—the Physical Plant people and the campus police—reported directly to him.

The meeting was over. All the bases had been covered. When, where, how, and why. Only one thing had been overlooked: what if . . . ? Curiously enough, no one stopped to think about the consequences if, as was a dead certainty, some of the students refused to leave. In retrospect Constantine saw this as "a major gap in our planning discussion," a gap for which he took personal responsibility.

I can only guess why this aspect of events was not covered. Constantine thought, somewhat naively, that the students would simply lay down their arms. He never thought any arrests would come to pass. I can't speak for Bill, of course, but my guess is that like Rhett Butler in *Gone with the Wind*, he didn't give a damn. Others in the room—I am certain of at least one of them—thought, "These guys must know what they're doing. They're the experts. I'll leave it to them."

What about me? Why didn't I speak up about the consequences? There is a famous set of experiments in the psychological literature—the Asch independence and conformity studies—that shed some light on this. A subject goes into a lab where there are several other people. Unbeknownst to the subject, all the others are plants. The experimenter shows the group two pictures, one with one line and the second with three lines of varying lengths. She asks the group which line in the second picture matches the line in the first picture. Which one matches is perfectly obvious. Yet the plants all deny that the obvious pairing is the right one. In a significant number of trials the subject eventually sides with the plants, agreeing with the majority that two lines of unequal length are, in fact, of the same length. Then the experimenter changes the conditions. Instead of one subject, she introduces two subjects into the lab. Now when the pictures are displayed, each subject has an ally in the other. In a significant number of trials they stand their ground regardless of what the majority says.

I didn't speak up because I had no ally. I had lost on dismantling. I had lost on delay. So I shut up on consequences. Constantine held himself responsible for what was to come. I suppose I did, too. Had I been a stronger person, things might have gone differently. But then, if my grandmother had had wheels, she might have been a bus.

When the Thursday evening meeting ended, I was left with nothing to do. I would have loved to have stayed out of the whole thing and just let events take their own course. I couldn't do that. It seemed to me that if we were going to take this action, then the least I could do was be there, if only to watch. Frankly, I'm not sure why I was there. I guess I thought it was cowardly to stay away.

The next morning things did not go like clockwork. As in a Salvador Dali painting, the clock exploded. The Physical Plant workers started to dismantle unoccupied shanties around 6:45 a.m. Some of the students occupying the shanties overnight were asked to remove their belongings. They did. Then some of the CAA leaders showed up. One of them was Arnold Contreras, an extremely articulate and effective protest leader, especially when things were hanging by a thread, when the action could go either way. Urged on by Contreras, the students started rebuilding the shanties, trying to replace panels the Physical Plant workers had sprung loose. Five students climbed on top of one remaining shanty. That's when Bill Dickson was called in. He gave a trespass warning. The students had five minutes to clear out. Here is an account of the action from the *Tech*'s special edition published the next day:

"There is a clear danger to the students," shouted Contreras as the workers approached the shanty. After a moment, the physical plant workers backed away from the shanty, and Campus Police loosely surrounded it.

"Why is it that MIT administrators won't get their hands dirty?" asked Contreras. "They make their workers do all the dirty work."

Dickson walked up to the coalition members and stated: "You have been asked to leave this site. You have five minutes to get off or you will be trespassing and subject to arrest."

Rosen [one of the coalition leaders] replied from the roof: "Why don't you do this in front of the students? Why don't you do this in the middle of the day?"

"This is not the end," said Rosen.

"I know," replied Dickson.

Twelve minutes later Bill Dickson gave a second trespass warning. More yelling. Then the campus police stepped in and arrested three students standing on the ground and five who were sitting on top of the only remaining shanty. The cover picture of the special edition of the *Tech* shows Arnold Contreras being hand-cuffed, his arms behind his back, a campus policeman with the manacles in his hands.

As the students were led to the police vans, one of them passed Walter Milne, an aide to six MIT presidents and a close friend of Paul Gray. The student said, "I hope you have a heart attack and die." Fortunately, he didn't get his wish. Walter died of complications from Alzheimer's sixteen years later.

The exchange between Rosen and Dickson was prophetic. It was not the end. In fact, it was just the beginning. Four years later, almost to the day, there was another confrontation. The characters were mostly different, but the outcome was if anything worse.

12 The Aftermath

At Olympic skating competitions, the skaters perform. Then the judges hold up their scorecards. That is pretty much how faculty governance works at MIT. The senior administration performs. When they do something really big like dismantling an academic department or a shantytown, the faculty votes. So it was that five days after the administration dismantled Alexandra Township and arrested eight students, the faculty held up its scorecard.

Faculty meetings typically began at 3:15 p.m. on the third Wednesday of every month during the school year. At 2:30 on the afternoon of Wednesday, March 19, 1986, just forty-five minutes before the start of that month's meeting, thirty protesters suddenly appeared in the corridor outside the president's office. It was an impromptu sit-in. I was in my office. When I got the news, I went to the protest. It was just around the corner and down the hall. I didn't want to go. I hated confrontation. I still do. But I didn't see how I could let Constantine face the protesters alone. Several of the students knew me personally. They were graduates in my department. When they made their accusations, they would look directly at me as if somehow I were to blame for apartheid, dirty investments, the arrests, the whole nine yards. I hated that, too.

"You know MIT is in the wrong," said one young woman who a few years later finished her PhD in linguistics. "Come and sit down with us."

What do you do in a situation like that? I had voted for divestment. I thought the shantytown protesters shouldn't have been arrested. I was on their side. But I stayed standing.

"I think it will be possible to dismiss the charges," I said to Constantine, changing the subject.

"I'm not so sure," he replied.

So here I was not sitting down with the students and not in line with the administration. I should have stayed in my office.

Constantine and I extricated ourselves at 3:15 p.m., offering the faculty meeting as our excuse. Lou Menand, a senior lecturer in political science and a long-time Institute liberal, brought the arrests to the attention of the faculty. I don't remember how. Maybe he raised it under "New Business."

Here are some of the comments that were captured by the *Tech* reporter:

"This is the first time in 14 years that there has been an arrest on the MIT campus," Menand said. "Once again, communication has been replaced by paddy wagons and police." Menand said he was shocked by . . . MIT's actions toward the students and that the arrests gave criminal records to the protesters. He concluded by calling on the faculty to address the issue.

Louis D. Smullin '39, professor of electrical engineering, described the decision to remove the shanties at 6:30 am as "a knock on the door in the middle of the night."

Arthur C. Smith, professor of electrical engineering, wanted to know why no faculty member was informed of the decision. "I don't know how decisions are carried out, but I do know that I was not told, I'm sure that the Dean for Student Affairs [Shirley M. McBay] was not told. And given that the administration knew of the faculty vote relating to MIT divestment, I want to know why the decision was carried out to remove the shanties without any input."

"It appears to me that the decision was made by non-faculty members of the administration," said Robert W. Mann. [What was I? Chopped liver? SJK]

Six weeks after the arrests, this statement appeared in the *Student*, a radical student newspaper, under the title "In Solidarity With the Working Class and Poor": "Keyser was responsible for brutally arresting eight MIT students who were protesting apartheid on campus" (April 29, 1986). I had gone from bystander to perpetrator in a month and a half. Role compliance was in full bloom.

The faculty agreed to reconvene in an extraordinary meeting on April 3 to discuss a resolution directing the administration to drop all charges against the students. A thoughtful letter from Matthew Bunn, a research fellow at the Institute, appeared in the April 1, 1986, issue of the *Tech*, two days before that meeting. The letter, addressed to Constantine, Bill Dickson, and me, said in part:

In the meeting with the students in the hallway yesterday afternoon [that would have been the March 19 meeting], Mr. Keyser implied that he believed the charges should be dropped, if they can be. Mr. Simonides, on the other hand, said he had questions about whether the charges should be dropped, because he wondered whether MIT should be in the position of asking the Commonwealth of Massachusetts to take an action, and then asking them to reverse it.

So here were the associate provost of MIT and the vice president giving conflicting views to thirty students who were sitting in protest outside the president's office a few minutes before the first faculty meeting after the arrests was about to take place. This does not seem like the actions of an administration that knew what it was doing. And, in fact, it didn't. As Constantine made clear subsequently in a memorandum to himself, "If I knew on March 13 what I know now about exactly what follows an arrest, I might have at least raised the question of dropping charges upon arraignment, thereby shutting off any residual effects, once the action of removing the shanties was accomplished."

I had been in my job for less than a year. This experience was an eye-opener. Here was one of the world's greatest institutions of science. Its faculty was world class. And yet we were rank amateurs when it came to this sort of thing. Why was that, I wondered? If these students had staged a sit-in in the lobby of IBM, they wouldn't have had a hope in hell of surviving the night as free citizens. In fact, just such a sit-in took place only four days after the March 19 meeting.

From the *New York Times*, March 23, 1986:

A Business Decision

Officials at the International Business Machines Corporation's offices in Providence, R.I., reacted straight-forwardly last week to an anti-apartheid sit-in by 14 college students: They called the police, and the students were arrested and charged with trespassing. A spokesman said I.B.M. opposed South Africa's policy of apartheid and for that reason considered itself "not an appropriate target." In District Court in Providence, however, an I.B.M. manager told Judge Francis J. Darigan that "for business reasons," the company wanted to drop the charges. It was not clear just when I.B.M. learned that Amy Carter, an 18-year-old freshman at Brown University and the daughter of former President Jimmy Carter, was among the 14, or whether her participation had affected the company's decision. Judge Darigan criticized the corporation for its about-face and refused to consider the dismissal request immediately, instead giving attorneys for both sides until April 10 to file briefs. The students pleaded not guilty and were released without bail.

For IBM it was simply a matter of declaring that since they were against apartheid the students were being wrongheaded in attacking them. That was it. They had the students arrested. The employees didn't vote or hold up signs or protest themselves. It was I-Business as usual-M.

Why was it so easy for IBM and so hard for MIT? Well, here's one answer. IBM is in business to make a profit. MIT is in business to educate students. Its relationship to its students is much more like that of a parent to a child than of a boss to his or her employees. That's why the faculty is so forgiving. "They're just kids," the faculty says to itself. "They're young. They'll learn." The problem is that this parent-child relationship goes both ways. The students know that they have a great deal of leeway when it comes to crossing their parents. They spend an entire childhood and adolescence testing the limits of that leeway.

None of that changes when they come to MIT. MIT is a relatively nonthreatening place, compared, say, with the outside world. At MIT students can vent their spleens whether against their rotten parents, their unacknowledged and as-yet-to-come-to-terms-with sexuality, their low test scores, injustice in the world, and, of course, all of the above. This they do secure in the knowledge that the Institute will bend over backward to accommodate them because in the final analysis they know that the Institute sits in loco parentis. And one's own children are never the enemy. Well, hardly ever.

As I mentioned earlier in another context, in *The Brothers Karamazov* Alyosha asks, "Who among us would not wish to kill his own father?" I think that question would have resonated with a lot of MIT students in the 1980s.

It was no surprise that having engaged in an action that resulted in the arrest of eight students, many in the administration and faculty began to think, "My Lord, what have we done?" A week after the arrests, on March 21, this letter to the community appeared in the *Tech*:

To the Editor:

We are writing in the spirit of opening further the lines of communication between students, faculty and administration after the events of last Friday. As many of you may know already, we have received a number of requests, including a petition from members of the community and a proposed faculty resolution asking that the charges against the eight individuals, including seven MIT students, be dropped and that MIT pay court costs.

Before considering these requests, we are seeking legal advice on the courses of action available to MIT. We have also received a variety of comments and suggestions from members of the MIT community and expect that these will continue to reach us and encourage all of you to contact us should you wish to do so.

A number of lessons can be learned from this experience, including the need for more collegiality and better communication within the community about issues that touch all of us. There will be a special faculty meeting called by the Officers of the Faculty after the Spring Break which will provide another opportunity to continue the discussion.

Samuel Jay Keyser, Associate Provost
Mary C. Potter, Chairperson of the Faculty
Constantine B. Simonides, Vice President

On April 3, 1986, at the meeting designed specifically to deal with the faculty reactions to the arrests, the faculty held up its scorecard again. The members voted 59–35 in favor of a resolution that called for MIT to dismiss all charges against the eight arrested students. A bad score.

Now the technicalities of the law came into play. Six of the eight students admitted to sufficient facts for a finding of guilty. Their cases were essentially dispensed with. If they behaved well for a certain period of time, then the matter would be expunged from their records. They did and it was.

Two of the students preferred a trial. One was found innocent. This was Larry Kolodney, a member of the CAA who was present to photograph the arrests. The other student, Arnold Contreras—an active leader in the protests from the beginning—was found guilty. He appealed but eventually agreed to go along with the others, admitting sufficient facts for a finding of guilty. The judge imposed a fine of $87 and a $15 victim witness fee. Contreras had rejected this resolution twice before but in the end he said, "I decided that it was better to be a part of the political movement than to be in jail" (from the *Tech*, February 24, 1987). Contreras hoped his court costs would be paid out of a fund raised by an MIT professor for the arrested students.

In the May/June 2006 issue of the *Technology Review* this notice appeared in the "Class Notes and Course News" section:

Arnold Contreras passed away on Dec. 18, 2005. Arnold's obituary confirmed the following: Arnold was with his family when he peacefully lost his lengthy and courageous battle with AIDS. Arnold was a gifted individual with a brilliant mind, and he attended MIT on a full scholarship. He graduated with a dual degree in computer science and electrical engineering and enjoyed a highly successful career in the computer industry in Massachusetts. Arnold lived the remainder of his life near his brothers, sisters, nieces, and nephews in Houston. He died quietly, comfortably, and with dignity. His family was at his bedside; he was never alone. Arnold will be remembered most profoundly for his beautiful, brilliant mind and the endless devotion he always showed his family, especially his parents.

I couldn't help but notice that the day of his death, December 18, was the day in 1985 when the MIT faculty voted to urge the Institute to divest.

13 After the Aftermath

As they say in the movies, "Four Years Later." The arrests of 1986 happened close to the end of the spring term. The summer came and went. But the beat went on. In February 1987 the Institute sponsored a colloquium entitled "Ending Apartheid." A representative from the African National Congress was the featured speaker. He argued for divestment. President Paul Gray, on a panel, argued against it. But then apartheid seemed to fade from view, taking a back seat to local issues like pornography, harassment, and homelessness. As the student newspaper, the *Tech*, put it in its 1987 Year in Review issue, "There seemed to be an emphasis on community at MIT over the past year. Students were not protesting oppressive regimes located worlds away. Rather, demonstrations focused on the injustices of racism and homelessness, national problems which cannot be swept under the rug."

It is not difficult to understand why apartheid protests took a back seat, I think. Interest began to fade with the passage in 1986 of the Comprehensive Anti-Apartheid Act, a congressional act that, among other things, prohibited any U.S. national from making loans to South Africa except for humanitarian purposes. That act was one of the major nails in apartheid's coffin, though it would take four more years before it died. Other issues now seemed more pressing. Even so, while apartheid was dying, it wasn't yet dead. It was just a matter of time before it bubbled up to the top of the student protest agenda.

The occasion was a meeting of the MIT Corporation on March 2, 1990. By this time most but not all of the students behind the 1986 demonstrations were gone. Some remained on campus and then, of course, new ones appeared, this time with a vengeance.

What had MIT learned in the interim? For one thing it had learned that it was useful to have as many faculty members in attendance at these demonstrations as possible. The hope was that the faculty would act like oil on troubled waters. This worked some of the time. On March 2 it worked, thanks to the presence of people like Henry (Jake) Jacoby, chair of the faculty.

My account of the events of March 2 is secondhand, drawn from stories in the *Tech* and from conversations with people who were there. This is what I think happened. The Corporation was to meet at around 1:30 p.m. in the Faculty Club on the sixth floor of the Sloan Building. The protesters wanted to make their way to the Corporation meeting itself, apparently to disrupt the meeting and hopefully engage the members in debate. Ron Suduiko, special assistant to the president for community and government relations, was in an elevator programmed to take the members directly to the sixth floor meeting. Suddenly eight students forced their way in. Without thinking, Ron pressed his chest hard against the control panel. The students tried to pry him off. Ron wouldn't budge.

He was frightened. He was all that stood between eight angry students and the sixth floor.

His first thought, he told me in a telephone conversation almost twenty years after the event, was "Why isn't anyone coming to help me?" He went on, "I was really taken aback with the demeanor of the kids. They seemed so intense and angry. Clearly they were or they wouldn't have been doing what they did. It struck me that they were so angry in that elevator."

That realization led to his second thought: "What am I doing here? What am I? Crazy?"

I think that was a common reaction from people like Ron and myself who found ourselves having to deal with crisis situations involving student protesters and not having the foggiest idea what to do. We were faced with volatile student protest and scared to death by the anger of the protesters.

Before the students were able to get to the control panel, a mix of campus police and Metropolitan Police Commission officers came to Ron's rescue. They pulled the students out of the elevator. The MIT chief of police, Anne Glavin, reported that five campus police officers were injured. No students were arrested.

This was only Act I of the protest drama that afternoon. Act II followed immediately. Seeing that they couldn't get to the sixth floor via the elevator, another group of students decided to try the stairway. They bolted up the five flights. Jake Jacoby was right behind them. He was there both as a professor of management in the Sloan School and in his role as chair of the faculty. At the top of the stairway was a door that opened into the area where the Corporation members were meeting. A policeman, his back to the door, barred the way. Jake took up a position three feet from the policeman and off to one side. He was there to observe as part of the oil-on-water strategy and observe he did.

This is what he saw. The leader of the student group put his face right into the face of the policeman and started screaming obscenities at the top of his voice. Spittle from the student's open mouth must have landed on the policeman's face, but the policeman didn't move a muscle. He was completely imperturbable. So was Jake. After five minutes of unabated screaming failed to get a rise out of the policeman, the students gave up. They went back down the stairway, leaving Jake and the policeman alone.

Some twenty years later, Jake told me that he thought his being there had actually protected the policeman. Given the provocation from the students and the threat of violence, had the policeman been alone, things might have been different. Jake could easily see the policeman fearing for his own safety and taking some sort of physical action. But Jake's presence enabled the policeman to do precisely what needed to be done: nothing. Jake described the policeman as a hero. Both of them were. The business of two people being stronger than the sum of their parts that I talked about in chapter 11 was certainly at work on March 2.

Later that evening at a popular restaurant in Harvard Square, a number of the protesters from the Sloan Building were waiting in line. They were talking about the events of the day as they came up to the maitre d'. She overheard their conversation and asked if they were involved in demonstrations that day with Jake Jacoby at the Sloan Building. They said yes.

"Well, you leave my father alone," she demanded.

My own baptism by fire had to wait until the afternoon of April 6 when, as an observer like Jake, I found myself standing around waiting for something awful to happen. Things started out peacefully enough, evenly gaily. The students had apparently constructed a portable shanty off campus. They carried it down Massachusetts Avenue and set it down on the verge that separates the Student Center from the street. It was a clever thing to have done, that portable shanty. It had the touch of a hack about it. But no sooner did the shanty touch ground than a squad of campus police came marching in ranks down Massachusetts Avenue. When I saw them, a sense of helplessness came over me. Once again I realized that I was a character in a play written by someone else. Here I was, associate provost of MIT, and it didn't matter a damn what I said or thought.

Whose decision was it? The president's, of course. In the *Tech* of April 10, Paul was quoted as saying, "It was my decision to remove the shanty . . . not a decision made in real time on Friday but a decision made . . . weeks before, that if a shanty appeared on the campus, it was not going to stay."

So the wheels had been set in motion long before I got there. The toy shanty was brought in. The police started their march toward the "unauthorized structure." Then the protesters started to do their thing. One particular memory stays with me. Among the 200 protesters on the scene, a woman began to scream at the top of her lungs. It was as if a dentist were trying to pull a tooth without Novocain. I suspect screaming was a role that had been assigned to her, though I couldn't be sure. Whether the screams were premeditated or not, the effect was unnerving.

At 4:40 p.m. Bill Dickson, assuming the same role he played in 1986, told the students they were trespassing. They had twenty minutes to leave the shanty or they would be arrested. The keening started again. The tension ratcheted up. At 5:05 p.m. Bill announced that the protesters had five more minutes before the arrests would begin. More keening, even louder than before. Several students locked arms around the outside of the shanty. Others stood inside, chanting "This is not South Africa." The battle was joined.

The campus police began to haul protesting students into nearby vehicles ready to take them to the station house for booking and on to the courthouse for arraignment. In general the campus police and the Cambridge police worked cooperatively with one another, albeit with circumspection. Each rendered unto Caesar those things which were Caesar's. If the matter concerned MIT students breathing in nitrous oxide in a car on a city street inside the campus, then the Cambridge police were just as happy to let the campus police deal with it, even though strictly speaking the offense took place on city property. In this instance, however, the charge was trespassing on private property. The charge called for the students to be taken to the police station in nearby Central Square. I watched all of this with a kind of shoulders-hunched, hands-buried-deep-in-pockets fascination, like watching compelling street theater, but on a very cold day. These were MIT students. They were protesters, tormentors, in-your-facers, but they were MIT students. The campus police were herding them into Cambridge city police vans. It was 1986 all over again.

Suddenly, a young woman broke into my uneasy reverie. She was the wife of an MIT faculty member who I knew personally. She was from Morocco and had come to the United States to study at Bryn Mawr. There she had been involved in antiapartheid activities. Watching six MIT students being handcuffed and led into police vans was unbearable to her.

"You've got to stop this!" she screamed at me. "You've got to stop them."

I never forgot that anguished face or that voice. The entire event has coalesced in my memory into that single moment: the young woman screaming at me, "You've got to stop them."

Recently I had lunch with her and her husband. I asked her to recall that event. I had seen her maybe once or twice during the past twenty years. I had never talked to her about that day until we met for lunch.

"Why did you scream at me?" I asked her.

"You were a senior administrator," she said. "I saw you as a person with power, as someone who could have stopped it."

"When you screamed at me," I asked, "what did you see in my face?"

She thought for a minute before she replied. Then she said, "Helplessness."

Three days later, on April 9, another attempt to put a shanty onto the grass outside the Student Center led to a confrontation between the police and the students. A demonstration at the president's house on the same day did the same. All in all, the two days of demonstrations led to the arrest of thirty-two students. The confrontations had been rough. One student went to Medical, claiming that a policeman had "bounced my head on the ground."

The next day's *Tech* reported many hand-wringing comments:

Walter Milne, assistant to the chairman of the Corporation, was present at Friday's demonstration. "My basic reaction [to the events on Friday] was I wish it hadn't had to happen, and then given that people wanted to have a confrontation, I wish it had happened more passively than it had."

In reaction to the events connected with Friday's demonstrations, Faculty Chair Henry D. Jacoby said "I sincerely regret that we came to this stage and that students were arrested; I really regret that the demonstration was pushed to the [extent] of physical confrontation with the Campus Police. I feel it's very important to have expression of views on a university campus, [that is the purpose of a university], but there . . . [are] acceptable forms of expression."

Jacoby felt the leaders of the demonstration "stepped over the line." Jacoby felt that the shanty was a physical expression of the demonstrators' attitude. "It was an excellently architected building, the purpose of which was physical confrontation with the police."

"Once the students decided to build [the shanty], the arrests were inevitable," Jacoby said, because the administration had "decided they were not going to allow the unauthorized structure to stand . . . [and] students were not going to remove it."

    Associate Provost Samuel J. Keyser, in a reaction to the demonstration, said "I regret that the circumstances were such that arrests were inevitable; that is to say, the scenario was an inevitable one based on the fact that the structure was unauthorized, and [Dickson] had asked it to come down."

    Keyser noted that he was aware of Gray's decision that a shanty on campus would not be allowed to stand. Keyser "became concerned after the demonstrations on March 2, that they were rather rough, and I was very much concerned that the future demonstrations, which I fully expected to happen, could end in violence."

Andrew Fish, a former editor of the *Tech* and a student at Harvard Law School in 1990, wrote this under the headline "Arrests Reveal Intolerance":

Apparently, the administration learned nothing in the past five years. When the Coalition Against Apartheid erected a shanty at a peaceful protest on Friday afternoon, Dickson again ordered arrests—this time 26 protesters, including a black South African, were taken to prison for protesting MIT's investment policies. . . . MIT has sent a clear message to the student population that visible dissent will not be tolerated if it is not conducted on the administration's terms.

    Associate Provost Samuel J. Keyser said that "whenever students are arrested in a protest something has been lost in an academic institution." He was right on target, noting that "a big part of that loss is the sense of trust that must exist between all members of an educational institution if learning is to go on."

So far so good. But then Fish went on:

But Keyser was very wrong when he said that the 26 people arrested Friday "chose arrest" as a way of protesting. The students chose to build a shanty as a way of protesting; it was the administration that chose to arrest the students.

Fish was right on both counts. The students chose to build a shanty. MIT chose to charge them with trespassing. To me it was perfectly obvious that the students wanted to be arrested. Why give them what they wanted, especially when it would be so counterproductive? Why not just let them sit in their shanties and sing their chanteys?

To understand why MIT believed it couldn't do that, we have to go back in time three years to the events that came to be known as Tent City, USA. That was the name given to a spontaneous encampment on a twenty-seven-acre parcel of land owned by MIT. It was scheduled for serious development. Today the acreage is the home of Le Meridien Hotel, ten office buildings, four upscale residential buildings, and parking spaces for 2,700 cars. Back then it was an expanse of vacant lot and a handful of boarded-up houses left unoccupied for several years. On October 19, 1987, three years before the second shanty event and after a two-day protest that MIT's plans for the so-called Simplex property did not include enough provision for low-income housing, a shifting population of street people—somewhere between ten and twenty—suddenly put down roots in the shape of donated tents. They significantly named their encampment "Shantytown, USA." In the end "Tent City" stuck.

Starting October 18, 1987, the Simplex Steering Committee (SSC), a committee devoted to trying to stop the development of the Simplex site, held a weekend-long protest against MIT's development plans. At the end of the weekend some ten homeless people decided to remain on the site. One of them, Carlos Gonzales, told the *Tech* that staying on the land was his idea. He wanted to show Cambridge that homeless people could make a home for themselves if given half a chance. The SSC donated six tents and Tent City was born. Some have suggested that the homeless occupants of Tent City were unwitting pawns in a game called "Stop MIT from developing the Simplex property at all costs." Under this scenario the homeless were puppets; the puppeteers, Svengalis with their own agenda. Whatever the origin of Tent City and whoever the perps may have been, mayhem was brewing.

The homeless stayed in their donated tents for four weeks and four days, resisting the attempts of professional social workers sent by MIT to talk them out of their tents and into nearby shelters. A real estate developer offered rent-free accommodations for half a year. The offer was rejected. Meanwhile sympathetic supporters including students from MIT and Harvard provided free food, firewood, and blankets. On November 2 the Cambridge City Council passed a resolution in support of the Tent City occupants:

Whereas: There are homeless people living on a grassy land area of the Simplex site, and known as Tent City, which lyeth in front of 55 Blanche Street in Cambridge and living in tents and

Whereas: These homeless people on their own have been doing very constructive things: prohibiting drugs and alcohol from their encampment. From refuse found in various places they have built storage and cooking facilities; and

Whereas: They have established security for themselves and the immediate neighborhood and they have continuous meetings to help themselves get organized and think of ways to let society know of their need for decent shelter; and

Whereas: On the site they have constructed large works of art. They have "thrown out" individuals who would not abide by their laws and have cared for alcoholics who have "come by" and are incapacitated. In their midst they have erected the American flag. All this they have done on their own; and

Whereas: This is a rare occasion to see people who have nothing attempting to be constructive and attempting to make something of their lives; and

Whereas: It seems that we can learn something from this unusual situation; therefore be it

Ordered: That the Cambridge City Council asks the Universities of MIT and Harvard to send to this area the appropriate professors and scholars so that they may study the situation to see if there are things we can learn not only to help these homeless people, but all homeless people; and also be it

Ordered: That the City Manager send whatever appropriate City officials to this area for the same reason.

The thought of "appropriate professors and scholars" descending on Tent City for the purpose of study and analysis was something straight out of *My Fair Lady*. What was the City Council thinking? The resolution sounded such a congratulatory note that it's a wonder it wasn't printed on paper suitable for framing and distributed to the Tent City dwellers in recognition of outstanding achievement in the realm of civic affairs. Did they really think this was helpful?

Groups with conflicting interests—the City Council, the SSC, the homeless themselves, MIT student supporters—all tugged in their own separate directions. MIT was afraid of the consequences. If there were fights in Tent City or injuries or worse, it could be held responsible. It did what any self-respecting business corporation would have done a month before. It arrested the homeless for trespassing.

The backlash was harsh. Three city councilors labeled MIT's actions "outrageous" and "reprehensible." The *Boston Herald* quoted the Cambridge chief of police as saying, "Poor people. Who the hell wants to arrest these people?" Cambridge city councilor Alice Wolf accused MIT of acting in "bad faith."

A trial against nine protesters arrested on November 20, 1988, began on January 8, 1989. Almost immediately the prosecution and the defense crossed swords over a single issue: does an institution bestow "apparent consent" on those camping on its land if it does not take immediate action to remove them? In other words, had MIT given the occupants of Tent City a license to use the property because it waited four weeks and four days to remove them?

On January 11, 1989—three days after the trial of the nine protesters began—the Cambridge City Council removed the last obstacle facing MIT in its development of University Park. It approved MIT's rezoning petition for Simplex. MIT had agreed to provide 400 residential units including 100 units of low-income housing, 50 units of medium-income housing, and an open park area. So much for "outrageous," "reprehensible," and "bad faith."

Tent City dramatically demonstrated that "apparent consent" was at the heart of the arrest of the thirty-two MIT students in the shantytown protest of April 1990. More than anything else, it was responsible for MIT's unwillingness to allow the shanties to remain without an agreed-upon end date. The longer they stayed, the more MIT was in danger of becoming complicit in their staying. From the students' point of view, the shanties were a very clever strategy. As soon as they went up, the pressure was on for MIT to take them down. As soon as they came down, MIT lost the moral battle.

14   What's Going On Here?

It was the specter of "apparent consent" that guided MIT in 1990. There was no way MIT was going to let students build a shanty and occupy it for an indefinite length of time. You put it up. We take it down. That was the long and the short of it. The only problem was that nobody had bothered to inform me. I actually thought I might be in a position to make a difference, that in all those endless discussions about what to do there was actually the possibility of influencing the Institute's actions. Perhaps there was. Perhaps Bill Dickson wanted those meetings in order to see if there was any reason to change his mind. Apparently there wasn't.

On Monday, April 9, 1990, the second set of arrests took place at MIT. The effect was disturbing. Several of us thought we had to do something. So that evening Jake Jacoby, James Tewhey, associate dean for student affairs, and I decided in the interests of bridging the communication gap to beard the lion in its den. We walked over to the editorial offices of the *Thistle*, the most important radical student newspaper on campus. There we met with the leadership of the Coalition against Apartheid, the CAA. Our intent was to arrange for a wider discussion of the issues with a group of MIT faculty. We thought something could be arranged for the next day at noon. The student leaders responded that they wanted to talk to Paul Gray. Obviously, we couldn't commit the president then and there. We promised to try to set something up. What we didn't know was that while we were bridging the communication gap, the leadership of the CAA was taking the bull by the horns. They called the president directly and set up a meeting for the next day at 8 a.m.

The events of that evening took me back to the evening in 1969 when, as a concerned Brandeis faculty member, I crawled through the window of Ford Hall to talk to the black student leaders while they were preparing to drive around Waltham at midnight with Morris Abram, the university president. That experience made it crystal clear to me that I was irrelevant in these skirmishes. The battle was strictly between the students and the president. Everyone else was chopped liver. I think that was why I came to suspect the motives of the student protesters. The president figured too prominently in their battle plans. It was almost as if the fight were personal. If I played any role at all, it was simply as a stepping stone to the president's office.

I suppose there are some nonpsychological reasons for this. At MIT the president is extraordinarily accessible. Paul's office was just around the corner from 10-250, one of the largest class-rooms at the Institute. Students coming or going to class were bound to run into him. Not only that, he lived on campus. The president's house abuts Senior House, one of the Institute dormi-tories. To get to the office Paul had to pass East Campus, another dorm. Running into the president at MIT was commonplace. On top of that, the president chairs the faculty meetings at MIT, a tradition that arises out of the close relationship between faculty and administration. This business of accessibility is not trivial, I think. When I first came to MIT, I was invited to be part of a visiting committee at Harvard. One of the first complaints I heard was how inaccessible the president was. I remember that especially because it was in such stark contrast to MIT. I had run into Jerry Wiesner just that morning. We exchanged hellos.

But I don't think the accessibility of the president explains my suspicions. What made me question the students' motives was the intensity of their anger, the same intensity that Ron Suduiko felt in that elevator. It was omnipresent. It was reminiscent of the anger I had experienced from the students on the MIT Committee on Sexual Harassment—so thick you could cut it with a knife.

I know that sometimes a cigar is just a cigar. But from where I stood, the protesters were protesting too much. It was not just apartheid that rankled, but the realization that there were people in the world who could tell them what to do and get away with it—in other words, authorities. The protesters may have been forced to accept that truth, but by God they were going to make the authorities pay. And, to give them their due, they were very good collection agents. Years of sniping at Paul Gray's heels took its toll.

Of course, lurking behind a dislike for authority was Alyosha's question: "Who among us would not wish to kill his own father?" An accessible president, particularly one as avuncular-looking as Paul Gray, was an obvious surrogate parent to practice separation on. That was not in the job description. It came with a cost.

Paul once told me that during the last year of his presidency, he and his wife Priscilla had a sort of inside joke. Whenever they performed an official function, a dinner, a meeting, a presentation, they would look at one another as if to say, "That is the last one of those we'll ever have to do."

But there was another reason why I suspected the students' motives. I didn't trust them. They were agitating for a world in which people treated one another decently. But I'll be damned if they were treating those around them decently. On one occasion one of the protesters thrust a two-by-four between Paul Gray's legs as he was leaving an Executive Committee meeting in an attempt to send him sprawling. Small potatoes? Maybe. But it sure as hell wasn't decent potatoes.

One of the protesters set fire to the Senior House banner, the one with the slogan Sport Death that hung in the stairwell of Runkle during Steer Roast. It was several stories high and steeped in wax. The banner went up like a Roman candle. One of the Runkle residents used to get falling-down drunk every weekend. When the firemen got to his room on the fourth floor, it was filled with smoke. He was lying in a stupor on his bed. The protester could have killed him. These were not the kinds of people who instilled confidence in me when they declared that they wanted to live in a world where people were nice to one another. Every time I saw them chanting "Paul Gray. You can't hide. We know you're on apartheid's side," I chanted my own version: "Paul Gray. Surrogate dad. Whatever you say makes us mad."

As I mentioned earlier, the subsiding of antiapartheid demonstrations between 1986 and 1990 was set in motion by the passage in 1986 of the Comprehensive Anti-Apartheid Act, one of the major nails in apartheid's coffin. There was another nail, the ascendence in August 1989 of F. W. de Klerk to the South African presidency after P. W. Botha suffered a stroke and was forced to resign. By 1994 the African National Congress was in power.

And yet, on March 2, 1990, MIT student protesters organized an antiapartheid demonstration. The date was significant.
Precisely one month earlier, on February 2, President de Klerk
delivered an opening speech to the South African parliament in
which he announced plans to dismantle apartheid. None of this
deterred the MIT protesters from storming the Corporation committee meeting on March 2. From the students' point of view
their actions were justified by an unwillingness to trust de Klerk.
From my point of view what they did was comprehensible only
if what they were really protesting had less to do with apartheid
and more to do with growing up.

One year later things had changed considerably. Chuck Vest
became MIT's fifteenth president in October 1990. The following spring, on Saturday, May 10, 1991, he was officially inaugurated. Two days earlier, on Thursday afternoon, nineteen
protesters had entered his office to ask his support for a community referendum on divestment. The results of the referendum would be binding. Chuck said no. That night the protesters
occupied his office.

Immediately a meeting was called. It took place in a conference room just across from the protesters. Constantine Simonides was there, as were the provost, Mark Wrighton, and Jake
Jacoby, chair of the faculty and veteran of the March 2, 1990,
assault on the sixth floor of the Sloan Building. The chair-elect,
Kim Vandiver, was also there, along with representatives from
the Campus Police and the News Office. I was there as well. It
was a turning point, I think, in Institute negotiation strategy.
We decided, for example, to let the students stay the night. At
one point I even went across the hall to offer them dinner. They
declined, saying that they were going to forego eating as a sign
of solidarity with South Africans conducting hunger strikes.

There was a certain amount of tension building. The next day, Friday, May 9, was the day before Chuck's official swearing in, and here were the students occupying his office with its direct view of Killian Court. The office window was just above and behind the podium from which Chuck would deliver his inaugural speech.

Kim Vandiver was designated the chief negotiator by the group. His chair-elect status lent a necessary gravitas to his position and, in any case, he was a perfect choice: a faculty member with easy access to the administration. Being chair-elect, he had no formal duties to perform during Saturday's ceremony. But beyond all that Kim was easy-going and quick on his feet, and he didn't take the sit-in personally. As a friend of mine once remarked, he was able to leave his ego at home.

Friday night Constantine told Kim that it was crucial that the students vacate the president's office by noon on Saturday. Otherwise, there would be hell to pay. Think of it. The president of MIT would have just been inaugurated and he wouldn't be able to enter his own office. Kim agreed. Saturday at 8 a.m. the provost, Mark Wrighton—whose own office was in the same suite as the president's—informed the students that if they were not out of the office by 9 a.m., they would be trespassing and appropriate disciplinary action would be taken.

Kim went in to see the students along with three other faculty members, Phil Clay, now chancellor of MIT; Roz Williams, a former dean for undergraduate education; and Jean Jackson, professor of anthropology. Jean knew many of the protesters. The three faculty members also had something in common: all three had served on a committee formed after the devastating arrests of April 6 and 9.

The study panel, chaired by John G. Kassakian, a professor in the Department of Electrical Engineering and Computer Science, produced a report that began: "The freedom to assemble and speak openly is fundamental both to the political health of our democracy and to the intellectual vitality of our university." It went on to suggest that when the faculty chair got wind of a "contentious" issue involving demonstrations and confrontations that might lead to arrest, he or she should immediately convene an ad hoc committee of students, faculty, and administrators to discuss what to do about it in accordance with a six-step program:

- Be available to consult with involved parties.
- Assist with mediation where possible.
- Review the issues in contention.
- Encourage community-wide discussion of the issues.
- Serve as observers.
- Report back to the faculty.

In fact, as Kim indicated in his comments at a later faculty meeting in accordance with the final step of the six-step program, the suggestions of the study panel had been "field-tested" in Chuck's office.

Saturday morning Kim and three faculty colleagues showed up in the office. It was around 9 a.m. At 10 a.m. a TV news crew appeared in the corridor outside the office. They had gotten wind of the sit-in. Less than fifty yards away the inauguration ceremony was beginning with the traditional entrance of the academics led by the chair of the faculty carrying MIT's mace. Inside, the protest leaders asked Kim if he would let them back in if they went out to talk to the TV crew. Kim said no.

Then he said, "I'll make a deal with you. If I let you go out and get some good publicity, which is what you want, I'll let you back in. But you have to agree that you will walk out of here by noon."

Then Kim and his colleagues went around the room. Nineteen protesters were in the president's office at the time. To each one individually they asked, "Will you agree?" And each one said yes.

MIT had come a long way from arrests at 6 a.m. But so had the students. Protests are a dance. And it takes two to tango.

15 Recommendation 14

At 9:30 a.m. on June 1, 1987, I was standing inside the MIT armory (a.k.a. the du Pont Athletic Center) at the corner of Vassar Street and Massachusetts Avenue waiting for the Commencement procession to begin. I wore my academic robes with the deep blue hood that tagged me as a Yale PhD. Being associate provost, I was close to the head of the procession, just behind the major dignitaries of the day, the so-called Commencement principals. For this, MIT's 121st Commencement, those principals included David Saxon, chair of the MIT Corporation; president Paul Gray; honorary chairman Howard W. Johnson (he had been MIT's twelfth president and had served during the difficult period of the Vietnam War); faculty chair Mary C. (Molly) Potter; Cambridge mayor Walter L. Sullivan; and Father Bernard J. Campbell, a Catholic priest at MIT who, almost six months later, would appear at the Cambridge City Council hearings on whether or not to censure MIT for arresting nine protesters from Tent City. John Deutch, the provost, led the procession as marshal of the principals.

The procession began promptly at 9:45 a.m. Walking in pairs, we hurried across Massachusetts Avenue at the entrance to the Institute, regrouped on the sidewalk, and headed south toward

Memorial Drive. At the drive we turned left. About a hundred yards on we were to turn left again into Killian Court. Two thousand parents, friends, and well-wishers were neatly seated in rows of folding chairs waiting for us, some of them since 7:30 a.m. The early risers wanted to get the choice seats, the ones that offered the closest view of their children marching past. After the formalities of the morning—the invocation and the speeches—came the moment they had been waiting for. That was the moment when their own child walked across the stage to receive an MIT degree from the hands of the MIT president.

It was a golden occasion for them. In many cases it represented the shining end of years of sacrifice, of scrimping and saving so that their children might attend one of the nation's premier institutions of science and technology. This was the moment when the offspring of a cross section of America's social structure—mechanics, salesmen, and stenographers, as well as bankers, doctors, and lawyers—became actors in the drama of American technology and science. The Commencement was just as much about the parents as it was about the children. That is why the last turn of the procession, the one that took me off the city streets and into the precincts of the campus, made me feel as if I were queuing up for a root canal.

Just before we turned into Killian Court a small band of demonstrators from Cambridgeport bearing signs demanding that MIT stop its callous exploitation of the Simplex property began to yell and jeer at us. Some of us pretended to be deeply engrossed in conversation with our procession partner; some of us looked awkwardly at the ground as we wheeled to the left and on into the court. I scanned the demonstrators. Sure enough, among them were two individuals that I saw as "anti–Commencement principals." They were student leaders of the shantytown demonstrations of the preceding year, protesting right along with the Simplex property sign-bearers. I had a sinking feeling. Another student demonstration was about to begin. As it turned out, I was right, but I had no inkling what it was the beginning of.

The procession turned into Killian Court. The faculty and principals proceeded to the reserved seats on the temporary stage at the northern end of the court. At the front of the stage, like the centerpiece at a banquet, was a table piled high with diplomas bound in red leather. A huge white sail of an awning covered the stage, keeping the sun out and us in shadow, a blessing given the heavy gowns we were obliged to wear.

This year the guest speaker was Kenneth H. Olsen. An MIT electrical engineering graduate thirty-five years earlier, he had gone on to cofound the Digital Equipment Corporation. The previous year *Fortune* magazine had named him America's most successful entrepreneur. Olsen's speech went off without a hitch. Then it was Paul Gray's turn.

As soon as Paul started speaking, the sound of police whistles screeched across Killian Court. The noise bounced off the walls of the buildings. I didn't know what to make of it. Neither did Paul. At the first sound, Paul was startled into silence. The whistles stopped. He picked up where he had left off. The whistles started in again, slashing into his speech like a knife into a painting. So this was the next demonstration. A couple of dozen students and nonstudents alike were "blowing the whistle" on MIT's president. It was an unfriendly foreshadowing of the "Pop Goes the Weasel" hack that was to greet Paul three months later at the President's Convocation.

As we later found out, a collection of student groups and community groups like the Simplex Steering Committee and the

Green Street Tenants Alliance—the Coalition to Blow the Whistle on President Gray and MIT—had decided to disrupt Paul's speech. Their list of complaints included MIT's failure to divest, MIT's failure to increase minority student enrollment, MIT's inadequate pension plan for its food service personnel, and its proposed use of the Simplex property.

I was sitting a few rows behind the dignitaries when the whistles starting blowing. As the whistles squealed, a grim-faced Bill Dickson, senior vice president of MIT, picked up the emergency telephone next to him on stage. He barked into it, his jaw set and his face looking as if it had been hit with a blast of Arctic air. I couldn't hear what he was saying but from the look on his face my guess is he was telling the campus police to arrest the bastards. Whatever Bill said, the whistles stopped blowing.

The next day the two students I had glimpsed at the beginning of the procession into Killian Court were charged with disturbing a school assembly, a crime in the commonwealth of Massachusetts. Who knew? It didn't matter. Two months later the charges were dropped in what seemed to be turning into a tradition: MIT students protest; MIT brings charges; the district court continues the case without a finding. Court costs—in this instance $50 for each student—are paid by faculty donations.

The same students were brought before MIT's internal Committee on Discipline (COD) to face charges similar to those in Cambridge Court. That committee also found them innocent. The campus police had had their wrists slapped in two separate venues. Why? Ed McNulty, the campus police officer who took the whistle-blowing case into court, was quoted in the *Tech* as being unhappy with the court's disposition of the case even though he "conceded to the district attorney that only charging two of the several dozen whistle blowers might be construed as selective enforcement." In other words, several people had been guilty of disruption by virtue of blowing whistles, but the campus police had only arrested two students. The selective-enforcement argument swayed the COD as well.

The students had run rings around the Institute. They had disrupted a Commencement, infuriated a president, thumbed their noses at a senior vice president, given the fig to the campus police, and avoided consequences. No prosecutions. No disciplinary actions. Just bad feeling between the campus police and the rest of the MIT community. The whistle-blowing incident was just the latest example of a dysfunctional relationship between the COD and the administration. Earlier in the year, as described in chapter 7, the same committee had created a constitutional crisis when it found that MIT's pornography policy was "an excessive restraint on freedom of expression."

It was no wonder, then, that a little less than a year after the whistle-blowing incident, the then chair of the faculty, Bernard Frieden, asked Kim Vandiver, a professor of mechanical engineering, and me to review the policies and procedures of MIT's COD.

To quote from the report that Kim and I wrote, dated December 7, 1989:

The Campus Police have experienced a certain amount of alienation from the community as a result of their activities in the past two years in dealing with student protest action and the reaction of the community to their activities. One major issue that has created these strains is the "whistle-blowing" at the 1987 Commencement. The Campus Police brought charges against two students two days after Commencement and the COD subsequently declined to discipline the students. This left the Campus Police in a quandary since they believed that they were acting in accordance with good police procedure and, nonetheless, the community representatives in the form of the COD did not support them. Members of the COD believed that they had good reason for declining to discipline the students and that, to a certain extent, the Campus Police were themselves at fault.

Senior vice president Bill Dickson had forced the campus police to act at Commencement with that irate phone call from the stage. They obliged. A few days later the COD told the campus police to go fly a kite. They were left, to quote John Ehrlichman, "twisting slowly, slowly in the wind." The alienation of the campus police from the rest of the MIT community struck me as a dangerous state of affairs, particularly because the times were so querulous. We needed to do something. Any future demonstration policed by a force of disaffected campus cops was as desirable (and risky) as another hole in the head.

Something had to be done about this disaffection. This is how I set about it. In the two years I'd spent as associate provost, I learned that so long as I didn't ask anyone's permission, I could pretty much do what I wanted to. It was like the advice given to trial lawyers: never ask a question you don't already know the answer to. I turned that sentiment into a philosophy of administration: never ask for permission, since the person you're asking might just say no. So in the early months of 1990 I took matters into my own hands.

In preparing our report, Kim and I had talked to present and former members and chairs of the COD; to the dean for student affairs and to several members of her office; to the chief of the campus police; to Louis Menand, the liberal conscience of the Institute; and to Mary Rowe, Institute ombudswoman. On the basis of their collective wisdom, Kim and I wrote the following recommendation into the report:

Recommendation 14

Periodic meetings should take place between the Chair of the COD and the Chief of Campus Police, the Dean for Student Affairs and certain key individuals, such as the Chair of the Faculty, special assistants to the president and other members of the faculty or the administration who show particular concern, to discuss issues that might lead to points of strain so that advance consideration can be given. These meetings would enable the faculty and administration as well as the Campus Police to keep in closer cooperative touch with one another and thereby help to avoid the possibility of alienation that always exists in difficult situations.

I decided to implement Recommendation 14 on my own. In the winter of 1990 I called a meeting of a committee that didn't exist. The idea was to short-circuit the organizational chart of the Institute and bring key people together not in terms of who they reported to but in terms of what they did. I selected people with special insight into or experience with conflict resolution— the ombudspeople, the head of psychiatry, the chief of police, the dean for student affairs, the chair of the faculty, the chair of the COD, assorted associate deans, the vice president for human resources, and, of course, Constantine Simonides.

The first order of business was a name. Mary Rowe won out. She was inspired by the speech in *The Merchant of Venice* that begins, "The quality of mercy is not strained. It droppeth as the gentle rain from heaven." So we called the group Portia. I was never completely happy with the name because I've never been completely happy with the play. I see Portia as an establishment lawyer who gets Antonio off on a technicality. But the name stuck.

I had conceived of Portia as a temporary thing, a stopgap measure until the "time of troubles" passed. It didn't work that way. Some twenty years later Portia still meets every Thursday morning. The only nod to the passage of time has been cutting the meeting time from two hours to one hour a week as the crises diminished in the nineties. One of its members once described

Portia as the only committee at MIT that solved problems in real time. It is worth noting that the committee that worked this way has been and continues to be a noncommittee.

Obviously, Portia's members find something useful in these weekly meetings. After all, they could vote with their feet—but they never do. I have always thought of the noncommittee as an encounter group. The members come together, write on the blackboard an item that's bothering them, discuss it for an hour, and then go away. What they do outside of Portia is up to them. The modus operandi is very simple. No matter what position you hold in the Institute, you drop your title at the door. There is no hierarchy. Nor are there minutes. Whatever anyone says is confidential. We took a leaf from the Senior House book. What goes on in Portia stays in Portia.

I remember two particular instances when Portia showed its value as a buffer between the campus police and the rest of the community. The first was a few years after its inception. A week before graduation a student dropped a Molotov cocktail from the roof of his dormitory. It fell within thirty feet of a campus policeman. The chief of the campus police went to the housemaster of the dorm and explained what had just happened. She was understandably upset. The bomb had come very close. The breach between the campus police and the community hadn't closed. Portia, I think, started the healing process.

The housemaster easily discovered who had thrown the device. When he confronted the student in his room, the student readily admitted to having done it. He told the housemaster there was nothing anyone could do to him. He was about to graduate in a few days, hardly enough time for a complaint to be lodged. He thought he was home free.

The chief of the campus police brought the matter to Portia just a few days after it happened. Portia wasted no time in working out a solution. A case was indeed brought before the COD. The student was required to work a certain number of community service hours before he graduated. Because it was so close to graduation and because his parents were planning to attend the ceremony, the student was allowed to walk across the stage on Commencement Day. The president handed him a red leather folder. Only there was nothing inside.

There is a curious footnote to this incident. The student who had tossed the Molotov cocktail was one of the students who planned the "Pop Goes the Weasel" hack three years earlier when Paul Gray was speaking at the first President's Convocation. This was surely corroboration—if any is needed—that past performance is the best predictor of future performance.

Perhaps Portia's finest hour occurred in the wake of the Oklahoma City bombing on April 19, 1995. At 9:02 a.m. the Alfred P. Murrah Federal Building was ripped apart by close to 5,000 pounds of ammonium-nitrate-based explosive that killed 168 people and injured 680 more. Since the blast came two years after the 1993 World Trade Center bombing in New York City, the FBI's first thought was that a group similar to the World Trade Center bombers perpetrated the Oklahoma City catastrophe. It was not a far-fetched notion. One of the bombers, Ramzi Yousef, had connections to Al-Qaeda.

In any event, the air was filled with rumors that foreign terrorists were at work in Oklahoma City. That posed a real problem for MIT. What would the impact be on our own Middle Eastern students? The day after the bombing was a Thursday, a Portia meeting day. The then provost, Mark Wrighton, asked me to bring the question to the group. Specifically, he wanted advice on whether it would be a good idea to write an open letter to the community or to contact the Middle Eastern students personally. What would be best for them and for the community?

I put the item on the blackboard that morning. Portia bounced the issue back and forth. At the end of the meeting I went back to Mark with a summary of the discussion: don't do anything.

Portia reasoned that there was a perfectly good possibility that the perpetrators were Americans and not foreigners. If that turned out to be true, any attempt to "reach out" would be an insult to the Middle Eastern students, no matter how well intentioned the administration might have been. Mark held his peace. The next day, Friday, April 20, Timothy McVeigh was taken into custody.

As it happened, Larry Bacow was a member of Portia by virtue of his being chair of the MIT faculty. Six years later, on September 1, 2001, Larry became Tufts University's twelfth president. Ten days after that came the September 11 destruction of the World Trade Center. Obviously, Larry had to communicate with the Tufts community. He wrote a letter that contained the following paragraph:

I urge you to not rush to judgment about those who might be responsible for these actions. In due course, we may learn more. However, even at that point we must continue to demonstrate respect and compassion for all members of our community. None of us condones these actions. We are one community at Tufts, and we must support each other in these difficult times . . .

Larry said it was his experience with Portia and the Oklahoma City bombing that guided the wording of this paragraph. Do not rush to judgment. Larry told me that in the aftermath of 9/11 not one of its Middle Eastern students left the university.

16   A Good University Is a Bad Business

Portia is a mechanism for handling crises efficiently, one that I would recommend to every institution of higher learning as a way of dealing with the cultural and behavioral upheavals that are unique to students away from home for the first time. They are attempting to acquire a decent education amid the background noise of growing up. It is a bit like whistling in a wind tunnel. But mechanisms like Portia are only the tip of the iceberg of what a university needs in order to run smoothly.

Like so many institutions of higher learning, MIT has to worry about maintaining an environment in which the best possible science and technology can be done while simultaneously educating its students and coping with their social and mental health and growth—not high-profit-margin items—and still staying solvent. Running a university is the mother of all multitasks. To put it differently, any institution of higher learning with dormitories, medical services, counseling deans, crisis management mechanisms, campus police, dining services, to say nothing of faculty, support staff, laboratories, classrooms, grounds keepers, custodians—the whole nine yards—is a lousy business.

Tuition at MIT typically covers less than half of the cost of each undergraduate. With a 4,000-person student body and a tuition of $36,000, MIT is looking at a $150 million shortfall with every incoming class. And that shortfall only gets bigger as costs go up. The economics of student enrollment at MIT is reminiscent of the used-car salesman who admits that he takes a loss on each car but claims he makes up for it in volume.

For the year 2009–2010 students paid $14,218 for room and board, books, and personal expenses. In addition they paid $37,782 for tuition and fees. This added up to a whopping $52,000 a year. You might think that only the really wealthy go to MIT. Hold that thought. For 62 percent of all students who had to fork over $52,000, MIT gave them on average $31,928 to help pay the bill. That's like going into a supermarket and buying $52 worth of groceries. At the checkout counter, the clerk charges you $52, then opens the company till and says, "Here's a little something to help you pay for that." His largesse varies depending on how well off the customer is (or isn't). But to six out of every ten customers he gives back enough so that the average gift comes to $32. (In fact over 90 percent of MIT undergraduates receive some form of financial aid, the lion's share in the form of scholarships, which don't have to be paid back. The situation isn't much different at Harvard.)

Does this mean that MIT needs to be run on sounder business principles? God forbid! MIT is not a business. It's not hell bent on making a profit. It is a place where the faculty tries to push back the boundaries of human ignorance and to teach students how to do the same. The faculty wants to attract the very best students, and the very best students want to come. The university does everything it possibly can financially to make sure that both parties get their wish. Profit has nothing to do with it.

A while back there was a lot of talk about reengineering America. It started in the corporate world and soon bled over into the

universities. At MIT it was a major effort for five years beginning in 1994. At the outset of the program several of us who
were in senior administration were called to a meeting in the
Faculty Club to hear what amounted to a motivational kickoff
speech. The speaker was Michael Hammer, who had coauthored
a book with James Champy, a life member of the MIT Corporation and a member of its Executive Committee. First published
in 1993, the book was entitled *Reengineering the Corporation: A
Manifesto for Business Revolution*. It was all the rage at the time,
and the Academic Council was brimming with talk about the
need to reengineer MIT. I recall very little of Hammer's speech.
What I do recall was one ringing phrase: "If you are not part of
the solution, then you are part of the problem." The quotation
was redolent of power and protest meetings of the seventies. The
tone struck me as appropriate for a regional sales meeting. The
academic enterprise wasn't even an overtone. One high-level
academic dean pointedly left early.

I couldn't believe anyone thought anything good could come
from looking at MIT through those colored glasses. Surely MIT
wasn't actually going to go down that road. But go down it it
did. Looking back a decade and a half later, it is impossible to tell
whether the enterprise was a dismal failure or a ringing success.
But either would be hard to prove. As far as I could tell, no one
had any idea how to evaluate what reengineering had wrought.

In theory the idea was to rethink how work was done. Not
academic work, mind you. That was sacrosanct. Reengineering focused on support functions: how MIT did its accounting,
cleaned its classrooms, and sorted its mail. More often than not
it was seen as upping the ante for those at the bottom of the
support staff ladder. One positive overview (from an MIT Web
site) described the following success: "The redesign of Custodial

Services resulted in the formation of 26 self-directed teams who are cleaning an additional 300,000 square feet of new buildings with no increase in the headcount. Weekday and weekend service were increased, again with no additional employees." From the boosters' perspective this was a victory for productivity. From the de-boosters' perspective, these "successes" were simply the result of increasing the workload at the bottom. From my perspective the so-called corporatization that so many of the faculty and staff complain about started in 1994 when MIT began to take seriously the efficacy of business-based strategies to cut costs. It did not, alas, take into account the impact those strategies would have on the morale of the working staff.

I suppose it is inevitable that every so often, like a plague of seventeen-year locusts, someone comes along with a plan to do something about the business model of a university precisely because it is such a bad business. Often those plans do some good. But never for very long. It's just a matter of time before things get out of whack again. As long as I've been at MIT there has been a budgetary crisis every ten to twenty years. Reengineering was introduced in 1994, and ten years later the Institute was facing a $150 million deficit. Well, you could blame Wall Street, I suppose. But I think the problem is basically systemic: higher education is an indispensible national need and a terribly bad business.

This should come as no surprise. In America there are businesses and then there are fire departments, police departments, hospital emergency rooms, K–12 education, and public universities. None of these are businesses. They are public goods. As such they are paid for by taxes. The citizens of Massachusetts pay taxes to keep the University of Massachusetts afloat. That is why students at UMass, Amherst, paid $15,000 less than MIT students for last year's tuition and fees. The taxpayers of the state were footing part of the bill. MIT isn't so lucky. I had always thought that state universities would be the Achilles heel of private institutions and that sooner or later the MITs of America would go the way of Bear Stearns. So far that hasn't happened. Who knows? It may never happen so long as the gift givers and the grant granters continue to do their stuff. But that is a big "if" and a thin reed on which to rest fiscal solvency.

All this talk of the fundamental insolvency of institutions of higher learning raises an interesting question: if MIT is such a bad business, then how did it get to be so good? It got by with a little help from its friends.

MIT is the love child of the War Department (euphemistically renamed the Department of Defense in 1949). As a result of World War II—and later the Korean War—the Defense Department pumped over a billion dollars (by today's reckoning) into the Institute during the forties and fifties.

A glance at the size of the Institute's faculty shows the impact of all that money. By the end of World War II MIT had somewhat over 250 faculty members. A quarter of a century later that number had quadrupled. It has been at that level ever since. One thousand faculty members. The number of undergraduates followed the same pattern: less than 1,000 in 1945; 4,000 in 1975; 4,232 in 2009. The Institute's operating budget increased by a third when the Korean War started in 1950 and by more than a third again the next year. The place was blowing up like a balloon. And even when the Korean War ended, government money continued pouring in. Sponsored research funds doubled every six years until 1968.

Somewhere in the seventies the gravy train slowed down. But by then the Department of Defense could boast of having created one of the greatest institutions of higher learning since the library at Alexandria. Now MIT counts 154 members of the National Academy of Engineering, 160 members of the National Academy of Sciences, 75 Nobel laureates, 33 MacArthur "genius grant" fellows, and even 4 Pulitzer Prize winners among its faculty, staff, and alumni—and counting.

MIT's endowment grew dramatically in the last decade of the twentieth century thanks to a spectacular flair for fundraising by it presidents. Nowadays, that is what presidents are supposed to do. But by the year 2009 it had taken a big hit, dropping 20.7 percent from $10.1 billion to $8.0 billion. By the end of the first decade of the twenty-first century MIT was showing a huge deficit, something on the order of $150 million. Certainly a good part of the reason was the blow to the endowment caused by the collapse of the subprime mortgage market. There was great irony in this since the theory behind derivatives was the brainchild of Fischer Black and Myron Scholes in a 1973 paper written while they were both at MIT's Sloan School of Management. As you sow, so shall you reap.

The impact on the Institute was palpable. There were close to a hundred layoffs the first year of the Institute's response to the downturn, 2008, and lots of grousing about corporatization. Many MIT faculty members saw themselves as having been sentenced to death by a thousand cuts. It was a reference to the increased number of forms to be filled out, requisitions to be sent in, parking fees to be paid. One of the least significant but most irksome changes was the label "employee" that began to appear on every new issue of a faculty member's identification card. To many, this was rubbing the faculty's nose in it. You work for us. We don't work for you. In fact, it was simply the result of moving to a new system of color-coding in which the system programmers had omitted the category "faculty." It was an inadvertent reclassification. But it had an impact. History often takes abrupt turns on the basis of such inadvertencies.

Who works for whom at a university is always a tricky question. After all, it is the faculty at MIT that decides who it will hire and who it will fire, at least when it comes to faculty. It is the faculty that decides what students to admit, holding a majority of seats on the Committee on Undergraduate Admissions and Financial Aid. Faculty members hold the exclusive key to graduate student admission. It is up to them to decide what to teach, when to teach it, and how to teach it. This certainly sounds like the faculty runs the place. On the other hand, it is the administration that decided the Institute budget would be cut by $50 million in 2008 and again in 2009. So MIT as an institution of higher learning displays an interesting division of labor. The faculty does the education. The administration does the numbers. So who is running the place?

The éminence grise of the Institute is undoubtedly the Executive Committee of the Corporation. Its eight members are the ones who, I suspect, call the shots when it comes to the budget. They have approval power. I say "I suspect" because I have never been to an Executive Committee meeting. Well, that isn't exactly true. I was invited to one early in my career as associate provost. John Deutch was provost at the time. During a discussion about changes in the Institute curriculum, Constantine Simonides, who was sitting next to me, got up to get a cup of coffee and asked me if I would like one as well. I hadn't known Constantine for very long. I was touched by the politeness of the gesture. I nodded yes. Constantine had an ulterior motive. He almost always had an ulterior motive, something I learned later when we became friends. In this case he returned and handed me the coffee, placing himself strategically between me and one of the Corporation members to whom I had just been speaking,

"His name is Cabot," Constantine hissed. "Not Lodge."

I had been addressing my comments of the morning to Mr. Lodge, undoubtedly confused by my inaccurate version of the quatrain:

And this is good old Boston,
The home of the bean and the cod,
Where the Lodges talk only to Cabots,
And the Cabots talk only to God.

(In the original version it was "Lowells," not "Lodges." But I wasn't from Boston.)

Maybe that's why I was never invited back to another Executive Committee meeting. Still, once was enough to get the message that these were the people who held the fiduciary reins of the MIT Clydesdales. They were the ones who could say "Hold your horses!" when the economic times were not flush.

So MIT is really a "shared governance" kind of place. The faculty makes all the personnel decisions. The Corporation, through the megaphone of its academic administrators, the president and the provost, controls the budget.

MIT's revenue stream, such as it is, does not depend on profit. To help feed its education and research habit, it depends on gifts from alumni and other angels who never even went here—Bill Gates, for example. Add to that foundation grants, government contracts (even foreign governments), and of course, a continuing flow from the endowment and you get some idea of where the money comes from. What this comes down to is that MIT is kept afloat by its good name. Industry, individuals, the government all support it because it is MIT. It is no wonder, then, that MIT's cycles of feast and famine mirror the same cycles in America. MIT is like a chameleon. It takes on the coloration of the economy it finds itself in.

17 They Are Us

While the economy may be MIT's bugbear, MIT is its own worst enemy. Paul Gray said as much on September 26, 1980, in his inaugural address as MIT's fourteenth president. Addressing an issue that had long been a concern of his, he stated:

The pace of MIT contributes, I believe, to those centrifugal forces which weaken our shared central purpose and which impair the coherence of our educational programs. We must take care that we have the time and the commitment to educate the person—as well as the future professional in a specific field.

Paul's comment reminds me of the opening of Yeats's "The Second Coming":

Turning and turning in the widening gyre
The falcon cannot hear the falconer;
Things fall apart; the centre cannot hold;
Mere anarchy is loosed upon the world . . .

Well, perhaps "mere anarchy" is a bit over the top when applied to MIT. But Paul was talking about a real issue at the Institute, one that over the years he referred to as the "pace and pressure" issue.

Arthur C. Smith, a former chair of the faculty and dean for undergraduate education and student affairs, came at the issue from a different perspective. He was fond of describing MIT as a "praise-free zone." It was his way of saying that you should never do anything at MIT because you want to be thanked for it. You are bound to be disappointed. It is not that MIT is ungrateful. Rather, doing the very best you can and doing it superbly well is not something a true citizen of MIT ought to feel is deserving of thanks. It is a bit like wanting to be thanked for being honest.

Ann Friedlaender, a dear and long-departed dean of the School of Humanities and Social Sciences—the first woman dean at the Institute, in fact—described MIT students as seeing themselves as having enlisted in the "mental marines." When I first came to MIT in 1977, students were allowed to take as many courses as they chose in their freshman year. And this they did to a fare-thee-well. It was a macho thing to do, to see who could take the most subjects/pain.

Since the grading system in the first year was pass/fail, all a student had to do was pass a course, not necessarily learn what the course was about. Admittedly, students had a strong incentive for maxing out their credits. If they could collect enough toward graduation, that would translate into real tuition dollars saved.

The Institute tried to stop that practice by putting a cap on the number of different classes a freshman could take. Now students have found a way around that limitation. After their freshman year, some students have begun to double-book. That is, they register for two classes in the same time slot, hoping to be able to do the work in one of the two classes in absentia using the Internet, online problem sets, friends, whatever works. It's hard to see how you can address pace and pressure when the students are doing everything they can to up the ante.

Jerome Wiesner, thirteenth president of the Institute, had a different name for the MIT ethos. He was quoted as having said,

"Getting an education from MIT is like taking a drink from a fire hose." The characterization stuck. It even inspired one of MIT's more iconic hacks when, on December 19, 1991, hackers rerigged a fountain in Building 16. They placed a fire hydrant embedded in a concrete block next to a public water fountain. Coming out of the hydrant was a fire hose. It was connected to the fountain plumbing so that you could actually drink from it. Pictures of the hack are scattered about the Institute.

No question but that MIT is a place where students work extremely hard. But why is that? Paul put his finger on it in his address when he said, "The capacity and passion of our students for hard work reflect those qualities exemplified by the MIT faculty."

In other words, no matter what you call it—pace and pressure, mental marines, praise-free zone, drinking from a fire hose—it doesn't begin with the students. It begins with the faculty. They are meant to be world class in their respective fields. You can't overestimate the amount of pressure that puts on them to produce. Sometimes that pressure becomes unbearable and they buckle. But they rarely break. To the best of my knowledge, not one faculty member has died by his or her own hand, though I can think of at least three who might have.

As for the students, in the thirty-three years that I've been affiliated with MIT there has been on average one suicide a year out of a student body of 10,000. Though even one suicide in 10,000 is one too many, that is pretty much the average for student populations everywhere in the United States.

Paul's comment suggests a special relationship between the students and the faculty. I think he's quite right. There is a special relationship. If you were to ask me to sum it up in two words, those words would be "master" and "apprentice." Add to that a significant portion of the faculty who buy into their in-loco-parentis role and you have apprentices who aren't just apprentices. They are extended family.

The engine behind the master/apprentice relationship is the desire of the faculty and the students to be spitting images of one another, clones if you will. The faculty wants to clone itself and the students want to be clones. Perhaps the best external evidence of that can be found in the numbers. Typically 50 percent of the MIT student body goes on to graduate school. That's 500 students out of each 1,000-member graduating class. That number varies from year to year, but 50 percent is a good average number. And of the 50 percent who go on to graduate school, something like half of those get PhD degrees. In other words, MIT is a PhD pump.

Even though I retired from MIT in 1998, I continued to host an event called the Random Faculty Dinner. During each of the nine months of the academic year, I invited 200 faculty members. Each month about 25–30 showed up. I did this for thirty years. That was close to 7,000 dinner guests. As the name implies, they were selected randomly. Each guest list was unique. After dessert I would ask the faculty members what was on their minds. I recorded their concerns and reported them in a memorandum to the president, the provost, the chancellor, and the officers of the faculty. Remarks were never attributed. It was all completely anonymous. You might think of it as a back channel to the pulse of the faculty.

Over the years a wide variety of topics were brought up. If I had to make a list of the top five, however, undergraduate education would be at or very near the top. The care and concern that MIT faculty members lavish on their undergraduate teaching was a source of wonderment to me. It is in marked contrast to many universities where, especially in the early years of an undergraduate's career, teaching of elementary courses is typically handed off to graduate students. At MIT it is not at all uncommon to find its faculty stars teaching freshman subjects, including nonlecture sessions called recitations.

The incredibly strong bond between students and faculty goes well beyond what students are taught in the classroom. It shows up in the oddest of places.

Take the case of Star Simpson, a young woman from Hawaii who fell afoul of the law. Here is a short account of what happened. It appeared in the *Boston Globe* on September 21, 2007:

Star Simpson was charged with possessing a hoax device today at Logan International Airport for wearing a sweatshirt that had a circuit board affixed to the front with green LED lights and wires running to a 9-volt battery.

An MIT student wearing a device on her chest that included lights and wires was arrested at gunpoint at Logan International Airport this morning after authorities thought the contraption was a bomb strapped to her body.

Star Simpson, 19, was wearing a black hooded sweatshirt and approached an airport employee in Terminal C at 8 a.m. to inquire about an incoming flight from Oakland, according to Major Scott Pare of the State Police. She was holding a lump of what looked like putty in her hands. The employee asked about the plastic circuit board on her chest, and Simpson walked away without responding, Pare said.

Outside the terminal, Simpson was surrounded by police holding machine guns.

"She was immediately told to stop, to raise her hands, and not make any movement so we could observe all her movements to see if she was trying to trip any type of device," Pare said at a press conference at Logan. "There was obviously a concern that had she not followed the protocol . . . we may have used deadly force."

Simpson was arrested, and it was quickly determined that the device was harmless.

"She said it was a piece of art and she wanted to stand out on career day," Pare said. "She was holding what was later found to be play dough."

Ordinarily, the incident would have passed unnoticed and the court would have "dragged its slow length along" had not the MIT administration put out a "reckless" press release, literally:

MIT is cooperating fully with the State Police in the investigation of an incident at Logan Airport this morning involving Star Simpson, a sophomore at MIT. As reported to us by authorities, Ms. Simpson's actions were reckless and understandably created alarm at the airport.

On September 24 thirty students protested the Institute's reaction. Standing outside a meeting between administrators and student government leaders on campus, they carried signs with slogans like Question the Media, Wait For the Facts, and Support Your Student. The next day the students presented a letter to the chancellor, Phillip Clay, signed by more than one hundred students. The letter began:

We, the undersigned, are concerned about MIT's lack of support for students during recent events, even after the facts of a situation have become clear. Unfortunately, it seems that the Institute's first and last reaction is to distance itself from members of its own community instead of attempting to diffuse misleading media hype. This trend is especially disturbing given that many of these students are the same ones that have been lauded for their creativity and innovation, qualities that are recognized and encouraged at MIT.

The chancellor responded with a letter of his own that ended:

MIT has a long tradition of encouraging its students to be creative and to explore paths that others might not. Good science and good scholarship requires this. We will continue that tradition. We are also required, however, to remind students that certain public standards have to be respected lest transgressions of them be judged as reckless.

Clearly, the Institute was not ready to give up on that word "reckless." Moreover, like every good institution acting in loco parentis, it sagely replied with an on-the-one-hand and on-the-other-hand message. The administration had extended a hand to the students. Apparently it was the wrong hand.

For a significant number of MIT faculty members, the Institute's press release was like lighting a match to see if your gas tank is empty—that is to say, ill-considered. At the very next faculty meeting (October 17, 2007), a motion was presented for a vote:

In light of the Star Simpson event, we, the MIT faculty, request that the MIT administration refrain from making public statements that characterize or otherwise interpret—through news office releases, legal agents, or any other means—the behavior and motives of members of the MIT community whose actions are the subject (real or potential) of pending criminal investigation. We offer this resolution to foster mutual trust within the MIT community and to promote due process for all.

This was a serious rebuke. It was also a startling one. After all, a young woman had gotten arrested at Logan for wearing a T-shirt that lit up and carrying a "lump of putty" in one hand. This was Logan Airport, where 9/11 had gotten its ignominious start. No wonder state troopers armed with MP5 submachine guns were super-antsy. The administration had described her behavior as reckless. Well, if you think about it, it was. It was a bit like walking into St. Peter's on Christmas Eve wearing a T-shirt with a Star of David on it that lights up and plays Hava Nagila when you touch it. In the normal scheme of things this wasn't exactly your "man bites dog" story. But this wasn't the normal scheme of things. This was MIT. And this was the student-faculty bond on the line. In loco parentis writ large. The students and the faculty had gone parentis. The administration had gone loco.

One of the two authors of the motion, Patrick Winston—Ken Manning was the other—was recorded in the minutes of the faculty meeting as having "related a personal story of how, when he was an MIT student, members of the MIT community went to significant lengths to support him, and that this contributed to his perception of MIT as an organization that is akin to an extended family."

This is the story that Pat told on the floor of the meeting:

My own views were shaped many years ago when I was a 19 or 20 year old undergraduate here at MIT. It was October, and the previous summer I had purchased my first car, a Volkswagen, near the end of its service life. After driving it around Europe a little, I imported it.

Then, it occurred to me from time to time that I should think about getting it registered in Massachusetts.

But—I was busy.

Then one night, or rather early on a Sunday morning, I was detained by the Wellesley police. They were upset because my car's muffler didn't amount to much, and they became additionally upset when they discovered my license plates were foreign and expired.

I say "detained" but many years later, in the course of a routine security clearance background investigation, I found that I was considered arrested.

In any case, I eventually received a summons, and a few days after that, I got a call from Chief Olivieri of the MIT campus police. He asked a few questions, and then indicated he would see me in court, which he did. When my case came up, he asked for and was granted a bench conference with the judge.

I don't know what Chief Olivieri said, but I imagine he said I was a good boy; a good student; not inclined toward reckless behavior; but just a little clueless perhaps, a common characteristic of boys just in from the corn fields of Illinois. In any case, the judge chuckled and dismissed the case.

I've told that story many times to many people—students, staff, faculty, anyone contemplating a move to MIT. I use it to buttress my claim that MIT has always been as close to an extended family as an organization can be. . . .

What I want is for people everywhere to say that MIT is a place that forgives—when it can; that supports—when it can; and that weeps—when it cannot.

I don't think you can get a better statement of the MIT student-faculty bond unless you sing along to Sister Sledge's "We Are Family."

The discussion and vote on the original motion took place on December 7, 2007. Those for the resolution argued that the administration had rushed to judgment, condemning rather than supporting a student in her time of need. They criticized the administration's style as being more corporate than collegial. One faculty member, apparently assuming the transition from community to corporation was complete, argued that the CEO of the Institute was responsible for its actions and should apologize for having given short shrift to the principle of "innocent until proven guilty." Those against the resolution argued that the resolution would tie the hands of the administration, that flexibility was important in these difficult times.

At one point in the debate Paul Gray rose to speak. Because he was an emeritus member of the faculty, it wasn't clear whether he enjoyed speaking privileges. His right to speak was questioned. (He had sought and been granted permission the day before.) Paul was one of the pillars of the MIT community, a bit of living history. Even though he was emeritus, he still actively taught undergraduates at the Institute. That his right to speak in a faculty meeting was ever questioned suggests how deeply felt the issue was. Paul argued that the resolution was tantamount to making policy and that bad cases make bad policy.

In the end the resolution failed by a slim five-vote margin, 31 to 36.

The incident festered for eight months. Finally, exactly eight months after Star Simpson put her hands up over her head outside the terminal at Logan Airport, Susan Hockfield, the recently inaugurated sixteenth president of MIT, issued a public apology at the faculty meeting of May 21, 2008:

> President Hockfield next called attention to the fact that there were also some serious challenges during the past year. She said that she has often thought about Ms. Star Simpson, who was stopped by Police at Logan Airport last September. President Hockfield recollected the National publicity that resulted. She stated that the Administration regretted its public statement, that the decision to make the statement was rushed, and for (*sic*) poor choice of words. President Hockfield shared her profound appreciation of the Faculty for their input and for their role in decision-making. Furthermore, she emphasized that everything that MIT does rests upon the Faculty, and that she believes wholeheartedly that leadership requires alignment between the Administration and the Faculty.

To an outsider not privy to the special relationship that binds MIT students, faculty, and administration, all this might look like a tempest in a teapot. It was far more than that. A significant number of the faculty had been uneasy ever since the new administration took over in December 2004. "Corporatization" was a buzzword for "marginalization" as far as these faculty members were concerned. Compare it with the old MIT. Paul Gray had come up through the ranks. He might be president, but he was MIT's man in the president's office. Chuck Vest was an outsider who had earned insider chevrons as a result of standing up to the United States Department of Justice.

Unlike a great many universities MIT does not have a faculty senate. This is not a surprise in an institution where the line between faculty and administration has been deliberately blurred. Until recently the notion of "them" and "us" just didn't compute. The MIT system of governance is one that, in the words of a former chair of the faculty, Jake Jacoby, induced "wide-eyed mystification" in a group of faculty senate presidents before whom he tried to explicate it. A keystone of that system is that faculty meetings are chaired, not by the chair of the faculty, but by the president of MIT. To outsiders that seems like a paradigm example of the fox in the henhouse. At MIT it symbolizes the culturally held view that the administration and the faculty are kissing kin.

As I write this, MIT is undergoing a significant cultural change. More and more high senior-level administrators come from outside the Institute. They are virtual unknowns to the faculty. Among them is Gregory Morgan, the first in-house general counsel in MIT's 148-year history. He joined the administration in January 2007, coming from a private law firm in Los Angeles, California, where he numbered among his clients Warren Buffett. Susan Hockfield—MIT's first female president in that long history—comes from Yale University.

It is not surprising, then, that a relatively young "outsider" administration might misread the entrails. By labeling Star Simpson "reckless," they were labeling many of the faculty "reckless" as well. That's what happens in a culture where the faculty sees the students as themselves thirty years earlier. That's what happens when you tar a master and an apprentice with the same brush. That's what happens when the master and the apprentice are family.

Twelve days after President Hockfield's apology, the charges against Star Simpson of carrying a hoax device were dismissed— not, I strongly suspect, without considerable effort on the part of the Institute's lawyers. If she performed fifty hours of community service, if she avoided further arrest for any reason, and if she expressed regret, a charge of disorderly conduct would be dropped as well. She did express regret through her lawyers:

I want to apologize for the results of my conduct on September 21, 2007. Although I never intended to act in a disorderly fashion, I now realize that the shirt I created caused alarm and concern at Logan Airport. I am appreciative to the Massachusetts State Police for their diligence in protecting our citizens and apologize for the expense that was caused that day.

Walt Kelly's Pogo famously said, "We have met the enemy and he is us." At MIT the faculty version is, "We have met the students and they are us."

18 Chūshingura and Catastrophes

Whenever people asked me how shifts in the prevailing culture are effected at MIT, I looked wisely at them, tapped the side of my nose with my index finger, and whispered, "Chūshingura." They would look puzzled, as I knew they would. I gleefully launched into my explanation.

Chūshingura is the name of a historical event in Japanese history depicted in all sorts of genres—bunraku, kabuki, films, novels, ballet. It is a long, long story that can take several days to perform on stage. I'll put it into a nutshell. The evil senior lord Morono goads the good daimyo Enya Hangan into drawing his sword in the shogun's palace. Decorum seals Hangan's fate. He must kill himself. He gathers his retainers—forty-seven ronin—around him, lowers himself onto two tatami mats covered in white cloth, and just before slitting himself open from left to right with a slight uptick of the sword at the right end of the gash as called for by tradition, he looks at his chief retainer and says, "I resent this." That's all he says. Not a long diatribe about what a bastard Morono is and how he tricked me and how I should have known better, but there it is, and I hope you aren't going to let the lowlife scumbag get away with this. Nothing like that. Just three little words: "I resent this."

That's how important changes are often made at MIT. People who are highly respected in the community simply have to say, "I resent this." Lo and behold, something happens.

Here is an example. Somewhere in the mid-1980s Edwin Land, the inventor of the Polaroid camera, came to MIT to give a talk on his retinex theory of color. The room in which the talk was held, 26-100, was packed to overflowing. I had managed to squeeze my way into standing room at the very back. About this time MIT was rethinking the kind of student it wanted to admit. There was a view that the Institute should move away from highly specialized students in favor of generalists with a broad range of interests. Land had obviously gotten wind of this. He didn't like it. He began his talk that afternoon, not with a general introduction to retinex theory, but with a disparaging comment to the effect that generalists were people who knew very little about quite a lot, jacks of all trades and masters of none. Science, he said in so many words, does not move forward on the shoulders of generalists. Shortly thereafter MIT was no longer looking for generalists.

Here is another example. The Committee on Sexual Harassment made its report to the Academic Council in 1990. The next year I started an annual survey. I sent it out to MIT's complaint handlers, to all the faculty and supervisory staff. In it I asked the respondents to report on the number of incidents of sexual harassment they had to deal with in one year. In 1991 that number was sixty-eight. The following year it was twenty-seven. By 2001 it was eighteen. This was chūshingura. Why? As far as I was concerned, the point of the survey was not to collect numbers—though that was a desirable side effect. The point of the survey was to let faculty and supervisors know that MIT was taking zero tolerance of sexual harassment extremely seriously. The survey didn't say that explicitly. What it said was, "I resent this."

Chūshingura is one way culture shifts at the Institute. The other, more dramatic way is catastrophe. It is extraordinary how catastrophes move people off their assumptions. When I first became associate provost, I worried quite a bit about how MIT chose to house its incoming freshman class. As I mentioned in an earlier chapter, the process had a name, R/O, where R stood for "residence" and O for "orientation." The emphasis was overwhelmingly on the R. For a week or so students would be temporarily housed in dorms while they roamed around the campus sampling every kind of living group MIT had to offer: the dormitories themselves, the special interest houses like Russian House and German House, the so-called independent living groups, the fraternities and the sororities. Students who were interested in fraternities or sororities had to pledge one of those groups. Students who were interested in dorms had to state their preferences and every attempt was made to give them their first choice. The students loved this process because it made them feel as if MIT was treating them like adults. In 1996 a survey showed that 87 percent of the students were happy with this system, more than any other freshman housing system in the country. What was at the heart of the system was choice. Nobody told you where to live. You decided for yourself.

The system was quite unusual. In most universities and colleges freshmen were typically housed in freshman dorms on campus. They lived there for the first year, at the end of which they were required to move out to make way for the new incoming class. This was not MIT's way. You got to choose from the get-go and you got to stay where you chose.

Why was I against this system despite its obvious popularity with the student body? There were two main reasons, neither of which cut any ice with the students. The first was that the way the system worked, a student would essentially stay in the same dorm room for four years. That meant students would see the same faces for their entire undergraduate experience. From the point of view of an administrator interested in encouraging diversity, this kind of insularity seemed counterproductive. From the point of view of the students, it meant that strong and lasting friendships could be forged.

There is no doubt that this was true. It was true of MIT in the eighties and, I suspect, it still is—though perhaps not to the same degree—that when students who have graduated look back at MIT, they look back not to the Institute, but to Burton-Conner, or Baker House, or Senior House, that is, to their living group. A friend of mine, an MIT graduate, Mike Strauss, still maintains active ties with the Institute. He interviews high school students in his hometown who might be interested in coming to MIT. He even has an official title: educational counselor. He provides high schoolers with advice and guidance. He frequently attends events at MIT to keep abreast of the Institute and of his own field, materials science. Mike entered MIT as a freshman in 1975. We met when I took up the trombone after a thirty-year hiatus. We still play trombone duets together. Mike told me that for him and a great many of his contemporaries, the three most important points of connection after graduating were and remain (1) one's living group, (2) one's extracurricular activities, (3) one's major. In that order. Mike lived on Burton-Conner 3 for the four years of his undergraduate stretch. He got his PhD in 1985. Now, a quarter of a century later, he still meets once a month with friends he made while he was living on Burton-Conner 3.

The logic of the living group connection is really very simple. The students like where they live because they get to choose where they live. But I think there is something else going on. It came to me when I recalled walking up a hill on Professors Row at Tufts University in Somerville maybe a quarter of a century ago. It was close to midnight, graduation eve, in fact. I was playing the trombone at the time, along with a banjo player and a trumpeter. We were leading the senior class to the top of the hill where they were about to be addressed by the head of the Alumni Association. We were playing Dixieland tunes—"When the Saints Go Marching In," "Bill Bailey," "Cakewalkin' Babies," that sort of thing. Each student held a cup with a candle burning inside. It was an impressive candlelight parade winding its way to the top of the hill—a rite of passage. It was also a ritual meant to bind the class not to where they lived but to Tufts University. The next day they were going to graduate. Tonight the head of the Alumni Association was welcoming them into a new relationship. Tufts hadn't missed a beat.

It occurred to me that nothing like that happens at MIT, no parading with lit candles à la Tufts, no marching through campus the way Princeton University's P-rade does, the oldest graduates at the head, and each subsequent class falling in behind after applauding its predecessors until the youngest takes up the rear. MIT has no such binding ritual. Well, that isn't exactly right. R/O is MIT's ritual, a week-long ritual with elaborate rules for finding and choosing and being absorbed into a living group. The problem with the R/O ritual is that it binds the student, not to MIT, but to where the student lives. For a smart place that is, well, not so smart! No wonder graduates have always been on the short end of contributions to the alumni fund.

But ritual or no, it was the second reason that was the stronger negative for me as associate provost. During R/O week students visited not only dormitories but fraternities as well. Roughly a third of the student body ended up in fraternities. But the problem was that it wasn't enough that you chose a fraternity—the fraternity had to choose you. If you pledged a particular fraternity and they didn't like you, you were "flushed." The metaphor was especially opprobrious. Think what is normally flushed.

When I pointed this out to student leaders, I was met with indifference or else with rationalizations about why it wasn't all that harmful. One argument especially galled me: life has its disappointments and this is a good life lesson. I was supposed to swallow the argument that the students were doing good by doing bad. The system was a foreshadowing of reality TV shows like *Survivor*. I might even have been convinced had I not made it my business to talk to students who had been flushed and who seemed quite content with the dormitories they finally settled into. They were hard to find. They didn't want to be reminded. But those who owned up to having been rejected admitted that it was a bitter pill to swallow, especially in their first week at MIT.

The insularity, the rejection, and the inordinate focus on where you were going to live instead of the character of the intellectual community into which you were about to enter dominated the student's first experience of MIT. For a few freshmen that first experience was rejection. I'm not sure how many there were. As far as I was concerned, one was too many.

Perhaps to stop me from harping continually on the unsatisfactory nature of R/O, John Deutch, much to his credit, formed the Freshman Housing Committee in 1989 to review how MIT accommodated each new class. That committee validated all of the concerns I raised and more. In October 1989 they wrote their report. The very first recommendation was:

For the freshman year, it is recommended that all students be housed on campus.

The recommendation went on to specify that freshmen would live on campus and be distributed throughout the dormitories. Fraternity and sorority rush would be postponed to the spring. In other words, R/O week would be changed completely—and in my view for the better.

On November 15, 1989, the report was presented to the faculty. Faculty members were split in their support. Those who had been through MIT themselves or who were involved in undergraduate housing touted R/O as a positive experience, lauding the "strong bonds established in student residence." Choice was also high on the list of positive arguments. Others supported the committee recommendations. One faculty member (as I recall, it was Lester Thurow, the dean of MIT's Sloan School of Management) commented that other universities commonly housed their freshmen on campus for the first year. This exchange is recorded in the faculty minutes:

"Could the other universities all be wrong?" he asked.

"Yes," came a faculty reply.

Sometime after the November faculty meeting, John Deutch sponsored an open forum on the Potter Committee report, as it came to be called. It was held in 6-120, a lecture hall that seats 154. It felt like 400, the room was so full. There was a brief description of the report's recommendations and then the floor was opened to discussion. Overwhelmingly, the students present—those attending were mostly students—objected to any change in the system.

John chaired the meeting and listened intently to two full hours of rejection. At the end of the meeting, out of curiosity I asked for a straw vote.

"How many of you are against the recommendations of the Potter report?"

Every hand in the room went up, but one. That led me to ask, "How many are for it?"

Way in the back of the room, in the very last row, at the very top, on the right, a single hand went up.

I was intrigued. "Why are you in favor of the report? Do you mind telling us?"

The lone voter said, "I'm not in favor of the report. I always vote against the majority as a matter of principle."

I think John and president Paul Gray saw that there was simply too much opposition. Not only was the opposition from students and faculty on campus too strong, but there was significant opposition from alumni who had gotten wind of the report and waded in with e-mails, letters, and irate phone calls. Consequently, for the next eight years, nothing happened. The report was shelved.

But it wasn't just the opposition that caused the report to be shelved. There was something else. Five years later, on December 15, 1994, Larry Bacow published a report with the trenchant name "Report of the Ad Hoc Working Group to Review Past Reports on Undergraduate Life and Learning." An appropriate subtitle might have been "Or Why Do They Ignore Us?"

In the introduction to the report the committee elucidated its charge:

Many previous committees charged with examining aspects of student life have labored hard only to see their recommendations fall on deaf ears, or worse yet, to be actively repudiated by the faculty, students, or the administration. . . . When the work of a group appointed to address an important issue is not acted upon, the underlying problems that prompted the creation of the committee remain unresolved, if not buried. Moreover, after one group has dulled its ax on a problem without result, it is difficult for others to muster enthusiasm to tackle the same problem again, regardless of how pressing the issue may be.

And in the body of the report, where it specifically addressed the failure of the Potter Committee recommendations to be adopted:

The chair of the committee was a former Chair of the Faculty, and other members included the Deans of Engineering, Undergraduate Education, Student Affairs, and the Associate Deans for Student Affairs in charge of Residence and Campus Activities, and the Undergraduate Academic Support Office, the MacGregor Housemaster, as well as three undergraduates and three other faculty members. One would have a hard time imagining a better committee to review freshman housing. . . .

Notwithstanding the stellar make-up of the group, the Potter Committee's recommendations went nowhere. Students were outraged by the suggestion that their freedom of choice in freshman housing be replaced by a system of preassigned rooms. Independent Living Groups feared that deferral of rush to second term would threaten their viability. The Dean for Student Affairs, who was close to the end of her term, did not strongly support the recommendations. The Provost (also nearing the end of his term) similarly did not endorse the report, in part, because of the strong adverse student reaction.

The bottom line, according to the committee, was this:

In retrospect, it is clear that in spite of broad representation of different groups on this committee, it failed to build support for its recommendations. . . . The committee hoped that implementation problems could be considered after publication of its report. We believe this was a mistake. Any chance of having a serious discussion of these issues was rendered moot by the strident student response to the recommendation that rush be deferred to second term. More puzzling is the role of the administration's representatives on the committee. Even though five deans served on the committee, the administration never supported the committee's conclusions. Thus the deans had no more success than the students in building consensus among their colleagues in the larger MIT community.

In other words, the committee had failed to build into its report a plan to implement its recommendations. There was no help for it. The administration, faced with the "strident student response," was paralyzed.

Part of that paralysis had to do with not wanting a fight. At the time that I sat on Mahogany Row, the upper administration was not densely populated. There was a president, a provost, three associate provosts, a couple of vice presidents—not a lot at the top. Other issues seemed more pressing. They always do. When they have the luxury, administrations are very selective about their battlefields. Student housing was not high on the list.

There was something else. There always is. In loco parentis wasn't a faculty exclusive. Many of the senior administrators and those who had their ears were ruled by the same sense of obligation. Some even welcomed it. If the kids are happy, then we must be doing something right. If it's not broken, don't fix it.

For two years after Larry Bacow's report—now almost eight years after the Potter Committee report—nothing happened. It was business as usual. Then, on Saturday, September 27, 1997, came the catastrophe. During an initiation event run by the fraternity he had pledged, Phi Gamma Delta, a freshman, Scott Krueger, died. Here is an excerpt from the Commonwealth of Massachusetts's statement of the case authored by assistant district attorney Pamela J. Wechsler:

On Wednesday, September 24, 1997, Krueger and the rest of his twelve-member "pledge group" were told by their fraternity's elected "pledge trainer" that an event, traditionally called "Animal House Night," would be held on the evening of Friday, September 26, 1997. The pledge trainer advised these twelve freshmen pledges that their attendance was mandatory and that they would meet their fraternity "big brothers" at the end of the night. The pledges were told that they were to gather together that night at 8:30 p.m. in a designated room at the fraternity, watch the movie "Animal House," and collectively drink a certain prescribed amount of alcohol. Scott Krueger expressed anxiety about the event to his twin sister and to fellow pledges at MIT. Like most eighteen-year-olds fresh out of high school, Krueger had limited experience with alcohol before arriving at MIT and moving into an MIT fraternity.

During the first part of the event on the night of September 26, 1997, the Phi Gamma Delta "pledge trainer" provided the group of pledges with beer and a bottle of Jack Daniels whiskey that he had purchased earlier. The pledges consumed all of the alcohol. At about 11:00 p.m., the fraternity "big brothers" entered the "Animal House" room and the pledge trainer ordered the pledges to line-up. The "big brothers" were introduced and then the whole group sang a Phi Gamma Delta drinking song that ended with the words "drink her down, drink her down, drink her down, down, down." Each "big brother" had an additional bottle of hard liquor to share with his "little brother." Scott Krueger's "big brother" presented him with a bottle of Bacardi spiced rum.

As the event wore on, Krueger began complaining of nausea, and lay down on a couch. Within minutes he began to lose consciousness. Two "big brothers" of the fraternity then carried Krueger to his new bedroom in the fraternity, placed him on his stomach, and positioned a trash can nearby. Approximately ten minutes later Krueger was unconscious and covered with vomit. Instead of immediately calling 911, a fraternity member dialed the MIT campus police who in turn transferred the call to 911. Emergency medical technicians responded quickly and discovered that Scott Krueger was not breathing, his face was blue, and he had choked on his own vomit. He was rushed by ambulance to Beth Israel Deaconess Hospital in Boston, where he remained in a coma for some forty hours until he was ultimately pronounced dead on Monday, September 29, 1997.

That was what it took to get MIT to revisit the recommendations of the Potter Committee report of 1989: not a committee report whose recommendations were, in my view, right on, not an administration determined to do "the right thing" regardless of the opposition, but a catastrophe. Larry Bacow, now president of Tufts University, was chancellor of MIT at the time. President Chuck Vest asked him to head a committee charged with redesigning the freshman living group assignment process. Here is a brief excerpt from the Bacow report:

In effect, Scott Krueger's death reopened a debate that had been going on for decades. As recently as 1989, a student-faculty committee—the Potter Committee—concluded that MIT would be a better place if all freshmen lived initially in dormitories, and if rush were delayed so that students could adapt to college life before deciding whether they wished to live in an FSILG [fraternity, sorority or independent living group]. . . .

Ultimately, the Administration did not adopt the Potter Committee's recommendation for a variety of reasons. Students and some alumni/ae opposed changes to a system that they believed had served MIT well over many years. They feared that requiring freshmen to live on campus would not only deprive these students of support traditionally provided by the FSILGs, but would also threaten the viability of the FSILG system itself. Neither the Provost nor the Dean of Students acted on the recommendations of the committee.

The death of Scott Krueger put freshman housing back on the Institute's agenda. In August 1998 Chuck Vest announced that as of the fall of 2001 all freshmen would be housed in campus residence halls. That was one year after Krueger's death. There had been a lot of discussion during that year, much of it with faculty and students, but much of it with a "hidden" constituency, the alumni. Many of them were angry as bulls at a May Day parade. I suspect they put the same pressure on Chuck that they did on Paul Gray and John Deutch in 1989 when the Potter Committee report appeared.

I can only speculate why Chuck finally made the decision that he did. For the five years before Krueger's death, I had been, as a colleague once put it, "a telephone off the hook." That is to say, having stepped down as associate provost in 1993, I had been out of the line of fire. Still, I knew Chuck well enough to know from a distance that the Krueger death hit him very close to home. He met with Scott Krueger's parents personally. That was probably the hardest thing he had to do as a university president, much harder, perhaps, than fighting the Overlap charges.

There was no way that he wasn't going to resolve what, in remarks to the MIT faculty at a meeting on September 16, 1998, he called the "unresolved" business of the Potter Committee report. The moral income he had earned fighting the Department of Justice over the charges that MIT had violated the Sherman Antitrust Act helped pay the mortgage on changing how MIT did freshman housing. Strengthened by the catastrophe of a freshman's death, Chuck was able to do what had been undoable at least for the past decade. He changed the way MIT freshmen were married to their rooms. It is significant that the president who made that important change should have been an outsider. His distance from the MIT student culture that that entailed may have added just the right dash of objectivity needed to do "the right thing."

How big a change was it? The biggest change in my view was that the week when freshmen came onto campus and settled into their accommodations was now a dry week. No more alcohol-soaked bacchanalias. That was a very good thing. Binge drinking is a form of sporting death, I suppose. That is what the Phi Gamma Deltas were doing to a fare-thee-well.

Binge drinking happens at almost every institution of higher learning in the United States. I read one report that said that 42 percent of all college students admit to binge drinking at one time or another during their undergraduate years. At MIT the figure is almost half that—24 percent. Why should that be? My own street-corner diagnosis is that MIT preselects for students who engage in addictive behavior. What MIT has managed to do is to channel that addictive compulsion into a nondestructive groove—namely, mastering a curriculum that is basically unmasterable. My advice to universities interested in cutting down on binge drinking would be to ratchet up the demands of the curriculum. I'm sure that advice would go over like a lead balloon.

What happened to the question of choice once freshmen were required to live in dormitory space on campus? As far as I can tell, they have the same amount of choice they had before, only it has been stretched out over a longer period of time. This is a crucial (and clever) property of the new system. The students choose where they live for the first year, so long as it is on campus and in residential dormitories. Sometime during the year they can choose to go into independent living groups in their second year or stay put. As of this writing, 50 percent of the male students opt for fraternity affiliation of one sort or another. The FSILGs, like good Darwinians, adapted.

What about the culture of the dorms? Judging from my 2010 conversation with the young woman from Senior House and from the (strictly student-made) DVD that accompanies the "Guide to Residences" that is sent to incoming freshmen during the summer to help them decide where on campus they want to live, the culture hasn't changed one whit.

That is a remarkable fact. If I were to walk into Senior House today, it would look slightly different from the Senior House of the 1980s thanks to a complete round of renovations in 1997, but it would feel exactly the same.

I think I know why living group culture at MIT is virtually impregnable, or, to put it somewhat less dogmatically, why MIT students are like right-wing fundamentalists when it comes to where they live, or, to put it differently yet again, why it took a catastrophe to blow the dust off the Potter Committee report. It bears repeating. MIT is a very hard place for students because science and engineering are very hard disciplines. There is nothing simple about Maxwell's equations or quantum mechanics or special relativity.

In 1925, when students dismantled and rebuilt a Ford motor car on the roof of East Campus, they painted the words "Tech Is Hell" across the roof of the car. In 1994 the initials IHTFP ("I Hate This Fucking Place") appeared on the license plate of the campus police car on the Great Dome. Plus ça change, plus c'est la même chose. All of this reflects the difficulty of the MIT curriculum and the finely balanced relationship between where students learn that curriculum and where students live while they are at it.

I mentioned at the beginning of this book that MIT's buildings are referred to in two different ways. They have either names or numbers. The way it works is significant. In 1916 MIT built E2. No one at MIT outside of a Physical Plant worker has any idea what or where E2 is. But replace E2 by its more common name, Senior House, and everyone will recognize that it is the undergraduate dormitory that surrounds the president's house on two sides like a boomerang. On the other hand, everyone at MIT knows where Building 6 is, or Lobby 7 or Building 13. The difference is that if the students live in it, it has a name. If they work in it, it has a number.

This isogloss is incredibly important in the history of MIT, certainly during the last quarter of the twentieth century when I was at the Institute. The name-versus-number practice represents a clear demarcation between them, the faculty, and us, the students.

For the students, where they live is a haven. After all, where they work—I mean, of course, in the classroom—they have precious little choice. The faculty determines the curriculum, and the curriculum in science and engineering is as rigid as it is unforgiving. You don't control it. It controls you. No wonder choice plays such a role in the mental lives of students. Where they live and how they live there is one of the few things they do have control over.

This protectiveness of one's living group is shared across the campus. In early November 1994 there was a rumor that the residents of Senior House and East Campus would have to move to Ashdown, a dormitory normally filled with graduate students. Almost immediately, a replica of the Senior House banner was hung from the facades of five houses across campus, with the Sport Death bowtie replaced by one that read Solidarity. Tire swings began to sprout on trees across the campus. The message was: maybe Senior House isn't for everybody, but everybody is for Senior House.

This has important implications for the future of MIT. Because being an undergraduate is so taxing, it is important that the students have a place where they can get away from it all. That means their living group. But because their living group is their first and foremost connection with MIT, it means that the kind of institutional loyalty that the Tufts Universities and the Princetons of this world are able to engender in their student body will always be just around the corner for MIT. If you look at the percentage of alums who contributed to MIT between, say, 1984 and 2006, it has fallen from 43.7 percent to 31.7 percent. That is certainly partly due to the economy, but a good slice of the blame belongs to the special relationship of where you live versus where you learn.

Still, something is changing. MIT hasn't seen a social protest of the antiapartheid ilk in close to twenty years. Social scientists have given the generation of students who shun protest like the plague a name, the "Millennials." They are the ones who followed the Generation Xers born between 1966 and 1980. They came on the scene between 1981 and 1988, the ones who fill the MIT classrooms now. They are the ones who were a twinkle in their parents' eyes while eight Gen Xers were arrested for building a shanty on the Kresge Oval. The Millennials don't protest.

Why not?

That is a hard question. I don't know for sure, but I will venture a guess. Here are two suggestive facts. First, according to the Pew Research Center, the Millennials are "more inclined toward trust in institutions than were either of their two predecessor generations—Gen Xers (who are now ages 30 to 45) and Baby Boomers (now ages 46 to 64) when they were coming of age."

The second fact is equally telling. When I was housemaster at Senior House, for many of the students it was absolutely anathema to call home. The antipathy that existed between them and their parents was rather like that between the Hatfields and the McCoys. The idea of calling home was laughable. During long holidays like Christmas break, Senior House was almost as full as it was during term time. This antihome attitude was aided and abetted by the so-called Buckley amendment, which made it unlawful for students' records to be made available to their parents. This was especially startling since, in many cases, the parents were footing the bill.

Here is a description of part of the sea change that has occurred between the generations. It is from a Pew Research Center report of 2007, "A Portrait of 'Generation Next'," about the Millennials:

They maintain close contact with parents and family. Roughly eight-in-ten say they talked to their parents in the past day. Nearly three-in-four see their parents at least once a week, and half say they see their parents daily.

In other words, in the past students brought with them to the campus a need to separate themselves from their families, something they had failed to do as adolescents. MIT offered a perfect surrogate father/mother figure to focus all the animosity and angst of separation. The protests were their way of completing the process. But the Millennials have no such need. Hell, they like their parents. What's to protest?

The young woman from Senior House who came to my office to tell me about the culture of the house today had a cell phone with her. It vibrated while we were talking. She excused herself. The caller was her mother. She was on campus and the two were going to spend the day together. This was the same woman who told me that in 1996 Senior House burned its constitution, an act she thoroughly approved of.

My guess is that the Senior House of today is a curious amalgam of the Millennials and the maladroits. They burn constitutions. They mud-wrestle. They watch pornography for free on the Web. But they phone home. For me, coming upon them now would be a bit like an archeologist coming upon an important fossil—say, Mary Leakey finding the tooth of *Australopithecus afarensis* at Olduvai Gorge.

There is another reason why there have been no serious protests for over twenty years. Students are too focused on getting a job, less so on getting an education. During a recent Random Faculty Dinner that I hosted, faculty from the Schools of Science and Engineering complained about the present-day attitude of students. In their view all they want to do is just what's necessary to get through a class. There's no fire in the belly to get to the bottom of a subject. Whatever fire there is burns solely for the purpose of getting through the subject and on to the next one and then, finally, a degree and "I'm outta here."

I don't know if this is generally true of the nonprotesting generation, but if it is, it will be a tough pill to swallow for a faculty whose motivation is to push back the shadow that separates what we know from what we don't.

19　"Hello, I Must Be Going"

Hello, I must be going, I cannot stay,
I came to say I must be going.

Groucho Marx sang that Bert Kalmar and Harry Ruby song in
Animal Crackers. It is my favorite Marx memento. It expresses
how everyone feels about a party at one time or another. It also
expresses how people feel about MIT. It's a helluva party in both
senses of the word "hell." As the students say, "Tech is hell."
After four years almost all students are glad to go. Not so with
the faculty. It takes a long lever to pry them out. Faculty members or administrators forced to leave don't go without a fight.
Of course, I am speaking about myself.

After I'd been associate provost for nine years, provost Mark
Wrighton called me into his office one day and told me it was
time for me to consider my future. His words came out of the
blue. Here I was, cruising along and suddenly a traffic cop
pulls me over. Mark was saying, "You've been in this job long
enough." Mark made it clear that this was his idea, not president
Chuck Vest's.

Mark asked me to give some thought to what I wanted to do
next. I was in a state of shock. "Do next?" I hadn't given it a
moment's thought. I had no idea that there was a time limit on

the job, though in retrospect I should have realized I couldn't stay there forever. There was no vice chancellorship in the offing for me. I was stunned. What in the world was I going to do?

I remember the precise date of this conversation with Mark. It was Friday, April 22, 1994. The reason isn't that the conversation had such a tremendous impact on me, though it did. Rather, it was because of what happened next.

As I always did in moments of uncertainty, I sought out my friend and colleague, Constantine Simonides. He wasn't able to see me until late in the day. He came to my office around 4 p.m. When I told him, he was visibly shaken. We talked for an hour. Perhaps there was something that could be done to change Mark's mind? Perhaps there was another job at the Institute that I might move to? Constantine was upset at the prospect of my leaving Mahogany Row. So was I. I was one of the few confidants that he had. Ours was a relationship forged over nine years of antiapartheid protests, pornography battles, harassment guides, Overlap battles with the government, and countless fires that we were called on to put out during the course of our tenures in office.

Our relationship extended outside the office. I had buried my mother in Mount Auburn Cemetery in 1985. Constantine was interested in finding burial sites for himself and his family. He turned to me for advice. We began making periodic visits to Mount Auburn Cemetery. It is the oldest garden cemetery in America and certainly one of the most beautiful. We would pack a tuna fish sandwich lunch and make the rounds of the graves. The cemetery's list of interred reads like a *Who's Who* of the dead: Mary Baker Eddy, Buckminster Fuller, Nathaniel Bowditch, Amy Lowell, James Russell Lowell, Bernard Malamud, Curt Gowdy.

Around 5 p.m. on April 22, Constantine and I parted. The plan was to think about things over the weekend and meet again on Monday morning to see what we might come up with. It never happened.

On Sunday morning, April 24, while playing tennis at Wellesley College, Constantine died of a massive heart attack. His tennis partner said he knew something terrible had happened when he saw Constantine lurch forward, making no attempt to break his fall. He just toppled over onto his face. He was taken to the Leonard Morse Metrowest Medical Center in Natick where he was pronounced dead at 11:35 a.m.

Constantine's death was so sudden, so unexpected, so monumental in its impact on everyone, that for a very long time we were all in a state of incomprehension. His wife Betty had rushed to the hospital that morning. She met her son Phil coming toward her in the corridor.

"He's gone," Phil said.

"Gone where?" said Betty, thinking he'd been taken to another hospital.

"No. I mean he's gone," Phil repeated.

Constantine and I never had the rest of our conversation. But perhaps we didn't have to. His death held meaning enough for me. That night I decided what I wanted to do.

I called Mark and said, "I'd like to retire early."

Mark was surprised. I suppose he expected me to return to my department and take up teaching duties again. That's what Paul Gray had done. But it wasn't what I wanted to do. Nor did life as an administrator outside MIT hold much interest for me. Oh, I had been offered the possibility on a couple of occasions in the past, but nothing attractive enough to make me want to leave the party.

I remember one invitation, from the University of Massachusetts at Dartmouth. The search committee wrote to ask if I would like to be considered a candidate for the presidency. I thought about it for a while. South Dartmouth is a beautiful place to live. Still, at that time I couldn't imagine myself anywhere except MIT. I said no as gracefully as I knew how. Six months later they wrote me again. In this letter they said they had been faced with hard choices in selecting a candidate for president, that I had many fine traits but in the end I wasn't for them. In other words, they were saying, "We wouldn't choose you whether you liked it or not." I took that as a sign.

I reasoned that going back to the Linguistics Department and teaching would simply be more of the same. I had been there, done that. I decided that it was time to try my hand at other things. I wanted to try writing, which is what I'm doing now. I wanted to try to become a jazz musician. I play trombone with several bands. I opted out of what I had done for the past forty years. I decided to live a new life.

Maybe things would have gone differently if Constantine had lived. Maybe we would have come up with a viable plan. Maybe I would have found another niche at the Institute. Maybe.

Not everyone leaves MIT like me, with a whimper. Many go out with a bang. Mark Wrighton, provost from 1990 to 1995, left to become chancellor of Washington University in St. Louis. Bob Brown, provost from 1998 to 2005, became president of Boston University in 2005. Larry Bacow, chancellor from 1998 to 2001, became president of Tufts University in 2001. David Baltimore, professor of biology, founded the Whitehead Institute in 1982 and ran it until 1990 when he left to become president of Rockefeller Institute. Because of his association with a colleague accused of scientific fraud, he resigned the presidency after just a year. In 1994 he returned to MIT at Chuck Vest's invitation. (By then the government had failed to prove a single count in its fraud investigation.) Baltimore left a second time to become president of Caltech in 1997. Bob Birgeneau, dean of the School of Science at MIT from 1991 to 1999, became the fourteenth president of the University of Toronto in 2000. Four years later he became chancellor of the University of California at Berkeley. Alice P. Gast, vice president and associate provost at MIT from 2001 to 2006, became president of Lehigh University in August 2006. Steve Immerman, senior associate dean for student life and executive director of Enterprise Services, was laid off in 2008. In 2009 he was appointed president of the Montserrat School of Art.

And then there is perhaps the most remarkable rise of all. David Ferriero began his career stacking shelves in the Humanities Library at MIT. He worked at MIT for thirty-one years until, as associate director for public services and acting codirector of libraries, he left in 1996 to become university librarian and vice provost for library affairs at Duke University. In 2004 he left Duke to become director of the research libraries at the New York Public Libraries. Two years later he became director of the New York Public Libraries, going overnight from heading up four libraries to heading up ninety-one. Finally, on November 6, 2009, he was confirmed as tenth archivist of the United States. Not bad for someone who started by stacking shelves.

These are the ones I knew. It is a remarkable testament to MIT as a training ground for college presidents and archivists. Of course, one might wonder why, if these provosts and vice presidents are so good, they don't make it into the presidency of MIT. The fact is that in the history of the Institute only two, Julius Stratton and Jerry Wiesner, managed to make that leap. (Paul Gray was a chancellor. Never a provost.) The reason is simple. One cannot be a provost at MIT without making enemies, enough enemies to ensure the provost's office is the end of the line inside MIT.

If MIT is hard to get into and even harder to leave for the faculty, the same is true for the students. It's a remarkable fact that MIT has no mechanism (or stomach) for expelling students. They can be suspended for indefinite periods of time. But the Institute simply cannot bring itself to say to a member of its student family, "You're expelled."

I've seen many examples of that. Students who have been caught stealing computers are suspended, not expelled. Students who stand up in class and wield swords over their heads are suspended, but not expelled. If you have cheated egregiously on an exam and are caught red-handed, you can expect to be suspended but not expelled. You can't even fail out of the place. I remember one student who lived in Senior House when I was housemaster. He came to me one evening and said he was thinking of committing suicide. He wanted to know what I thought. This was a student who'd gotten an F in every one of his courses that semester. You would think that MIT would say, "Enough is enough." But no. He'd just had a bad term. We would let him back in again next semester. This wasn't a kid who didn't get it. He was just a kid who didn't want to spend the time getting it.

"You want to commit suicide because of your grades?" I asked him.

"No," he said, pained that I might think something so idiotic of him. "It's my girlfriend. She wants to break up with me."

"Who is she?" I asked.

He mentioned the name. I knew her. She wasn't exactly a Miss Personality in my world but, of course, she wasn't really an occupant of my world.

"I'm thinking of jumping off the Green Building," he went on. "So what do you think?"

"I think she's worth jumping out of the first floor window of Runkle. But not the roof of the Green Building. She's just not in that class," I said.

"Really?" he said quizzically.

"Really," I replied. "But do me a favor. If you still feel like jumping off the roof of the Green Building, will you give me a call first so I can try to talk you out of it?"

Later that semester he dropped out of MIT altogether. I saw him just before he left.

"What are you going to do?" I asked.

"I got a job with a software house in Cambridge."

"How much are they paying you?"

"$60,000."

And that was in the mid-1980s for a kid who'd failed his last five subjects.

It seems appropriate that I end this book with an account of the most memorable escape from MIT of all—though, twenty-seven years after the fact, I seem to have been the only one to have remembered it. Certainly, the students of Senior House were oblivious. I had been housemaster for two years when, on October 23, 1983, one of the students in the house mysteriously disappeared. He had gone hiking with two friends in the White Mountains of New Hampshire. Somewhere along the path to the top of Mt. Lafayette the group split up. According to the New Hampshire police detective I spoke to recently, the student's friends followed the zigzag trail that led to the summit. The student decided that the shortest distance between two points was a straight line. He would navigate the dense growth that covered the mountain between himself and the top. Perhaps he realized that there were only a few hours of daylight left for a climb that normally took five hours. He was wearing a leather jacket, a sweater, jeans, and hiking boots. On this Sunday, though, the winds were gusting as high as forty miles per hour with temperatures around fifteen degrees. He was dressed for a walk along the Charles River, not for a hike up to a 5,200-foot-high mountain peak and a descent in the dark. He was sporting death with a vengeance. When his friends reached the summit, he wasn't there. They assumed he had turned back. They started down. It was late in the day. The Senior House student wasn't at the bottom either. Now his friends were concerned. It gets cold very quickly in the White Mountains.

A week after the student's disappearance the state police called off the search for his body. Lt. Brian Howe of the New Hampshire Fish and Game Department was quoted in the *Tech* (November 1, 1983) as saying, "We are absolutely sure that if he's up there, he's dead." I took note of the "if."

A month after the student disappeared a memorial service was held in the MIT chapel. According to the *Tech*, one of the speakers described his lost friend as having a tendency toward "recklessness"—there was that word again—someone who felt he could "get away with" courting danger.

Later that same winter a body was found on the mountain that was supposed to have claimed the Senior House student. Apparently the dead man was lost and had climbed a tree to get his bearings. He was found frozen solid halfway up the tree. The state police phoned the head of psychiatry at MIT to tell him about the body. The head of psychiatry assumed it was the missing student. He called Senior House and told my wife that the young man's body had been found. Margaret called his mother. But it was a false alarm. The body was that of another hiker.

When I recently phoned the state police in New Hampshire, twenty-seven years had passed since the student disappeared. The police detective I spoke to knew the case. He was a bit curious about why I was asking. It seemed that just before I called he had been looking at precisely that student's file. It was still open. The student was still listed as a missing person.

The detective told me it wasn't surprising they hadn't found a body. The trees on the mountain are what the Germans call Krummholz, literally "crooked wood." The warped low-lying growth comes about because the trees are continually exposed to the harsh conditions atop the White Mountains—unrelenting, icy blasts that force the piney growth into grotesque mats, thick and distorted. Like an arboreal version of Chinese foot binding, the trees end up stunted, deformed, misshapen. It would be easy, the detective said, for someone to disappear into that kind of undergrowth and never be found again.

Whenever I see the Sport Death logo, I think of this student. What a perfect candidate for the myth behind the banner. The detective thinks it most likely he is dead. But I had heard a rumor that he was involved in selling drugs in the dorm. If that was so, then I think it just as likely that he staged his own disappearance, that somewhere out there he is alive and well, a Senior House alumnus aching to return but unable to make the journey.